8/24

Target Eisenhower

Military and Political Assassination in WWII

TARGET EISENHOWER

MILITARY AND POLITICAL ASSASSINATION IN WWII

by

Charles Whiting

'My knowledge of pain, learned with the sabre, taught me just to be afraid of
fear. And, just as in duelling you must fix your mind at striking at the enemy's
head, so too in war. You cannot waste time feinting and sidestepping.
You must decide on your target and go in.'
Obersturmführer Otto Skorzeny,
Head of German Special Forces in World War II

SPELLMOUNT
Staplehurst

British Library Cataloguing in Publication Data:
A catalogue record for this book is available
from the British Library

First published in the UK in 2005
by
Spellmount Limited
The Village Centre
Staplehurst
Kent TN12 0BJ

ISBN 1-86227-285-9

Tel: 01580 893730
Fax: 01580 893731
E-mail: enquiries@spellmount.com
Website: www.spellmount.com

1 3 5 7 9 8 6 4 2

Printed in Great Britain by
Oaklands Book Services
Stonehouse, Gloucestershire GL10 3RQ

Contents

Author's Note

'*Der Plan ist geandert worden,*' the little Herr Doktor with the cropped blond hair and ready, if wary, smile whispered to me. A minute earlier he had arrived on the cold platform of the little provincial station, as if out of nowhere, pushing his way through the commuters, carrying their shabby, imitation leather briefcases which probably contained *Wurstbrote* for their ten o'clock snack.

The day before he had arranged the journey for me. The Herr Doktor with the impeccable democratic connections seemed to know everyone on the right-wing scene. I was to travel *alone* to Hamburg's main station, where one of the 'Great Man's' men would pick me up and take me to the suburban hospital on the outskirts of the port city. Here the 'Great Man', who was in the German Federal Republic illegally, would give me an interview from his sick bed.

Now, as he had just told me on this cold winter's morning, the plan had been changed. Our destination was different and he was coming with me. He didn't say why. Was it some kind of real life cat-and-mouse game? After all the Herr Doktor stood to lose his job in that staid publishing house, which would one day dominate the publishing scene in the English-speaking world. His employers enjoyed their new post-war respectability; they didn't want to be reminded of the Nazi past. Or was it play acting? After all this strange war in the shadows of which the 'Great Man', as the Herr Doktor called him, was part, had now been going on for a quarter of a century or more since the end of their lost war. The 'Great Man' and the rest of that crowd were, in reality, yesterday's men.

But I wanted the interview and didn't ask questions. So we set off in a crowded second-class compartment – 'one might meet someone one knows in the first class and that would be embarrassing, eh?' Now our destination was Harburg, a medium-sized industrial town on the other side of the Elbe river opposite Hamburg. I understood, didn't I? The man I was anxious to interview was still wanted in the Federal Republic ever since he had been smuggled out of the internment camp by three SS officers clad in American uniforms. After all, the 'Great Man' spelled

vii

trouble wherever he went. Besides the 'Reds' – the little Herr Doktor still used terms like that – would dearly love to get their hands on him. They'd probably give the 'Great Man' a show trial: an Eichmann in reverse as it were.

An hour or so later we reached Harburg. Outside the shabby station, a black BMW was waiting for us, its engine already running. I noted it didn't have local plates. In addition the big burly driver didn't introduce himself as is customary in a still very formal Germany, though he bowed slightly to the Herr Doktor.

We were hardly inside the car when the driver was off at top speed. For the next ten minutes or so it was obvious that he was driving round and round Harburg because I began to recognise places we'd passed a few minutes earlier. Satisfied we were not being followed, he dropped us off in a nondescript street and sped away.

The flat – in fact there were two of them for reasons I could never fathom – was crowded with big middle-aged men, mostly in shabby dark suits. It was obvious they didn't live here, for most of them were clearly foreigners to judge from their accents. Although it was only ten in the morning, all of them were drinking *Sekt*, the German sparkling wine, or whisky at an alarming rate. No introductions were given or asked for. Indeed there was something vaguely alarming about the whole set-up.

Finally, whoever was in charge – I never discovered who it was – decided everything was safe. 'They' had been thrown off the scent. He must have made a telephone call for within minutes, as if by magic, a small fleet of cars appeared in the street below. Off we went. Behind us tagged a battered Volkswagen 'Beetle'. Obviously he was 'tail-end Charlie' checking whether we were being followed.

As we crossed the girder bridge into Hamburg, I learned from the Herr Doktor why the 'Great Man' was in Germany. In Madrid, which had been his base since he had been smuggled out of the interment camp, his doctors had found two tumours on his spine, one on top of the other. They had to be removed at once and the Spanish doctors had said the operation had a better chance in Hamburg than in Madrid.

Now he lay in a private room at the top floor of a *Klinik*, as such places are always called in Germany, guarded by his ex-commandos who had come from all over Europe to guard their old chief. He had lost a great deal of weight. His face was a strange unhealthy yellow colour. But the criss-cross scars of his student duelling days were still visible and he still had that bold challenging look that I remembered from the photos taken when his exploits had made him world famous – some say infamous.

'Skorzeny,' he said in a soft Viennese accent. He offered me a weak hand and, although lying in his hospital bed, he even attempted the traditional Austrian bow from the shoulders – *der Diener* (the servant).

So this was the 'great man' in the flesh, albeit weakened flesh. In the mid-40s he had created a new kind of warfare. Unlike his counterpart in the SAS, Colonel David Stirling, Skorzeny and his men of the Hunting Commando had not limited themselves to military targets. Instead they had attempted to bring about major political decisions by attacking – even assassinating if necessary – major political leaders.

In 1943 it had been the rescue of Mussolini which kept Italy in the war. Later that year there had been 'Operation Long Jump' and the attempt to assassinate the 'Big Three', Churchill, Stalin and Roosevelt. That op. had failed. A year later Skorzeny had kept Hungary in the war on Germany's side by kidnapping the son of that country's ruler. Even Churchill had praised Skorzeny in the House of Commons and stated that the Austrian had brought a 'new dimension' to warfare.

By 1944, others, in particular Germany's enemies, were rapidly learning the harsh lessons taught by the scarfaced giant. Skorzeny's theory that one should 'go for the head and not the guts' was becoming standard operating procedure. In other words sever the head of some major enemy political leader and the 'guts', his state, might well collapse of its own accord.

That year, the British planned the assassination of the 'Desert Fox', Field Marshal Rommel, who stood in the way of their victory in France. Meanwhile the Americans were planning an even more significant assassination, that of Adolf Hitler. The old unwritten truce between Germany and the Western Allies was abandoned. Now murder was a legitimate means of winning victory, perhaps even the war.

In the years that followed that war, in the USA, assassination attempts were made on three US presidents, Truman, Kennedy and Reagan. Only Harry Truman survived without injury. In Europe there was little difference. Twice attempts were made by political opponents and terrorists to kill President de Gaulle. And in Britain terrorists attempted to kill not only a prime minister, Margaret Thatcher, but most of her cabinet too.

Today terrorism, our leaders tell us, is *the* major threat, not only to the western democracies, but to the whole world, democratic or otherwise. Now terrorism has apparently become the ruling factor in military and political thinking. Our Western leaders drum that hard, brutal fact into us daily.

The answer to that threat is all around us in our daily lives, a constant reminder that we are under attack. Airports outside our bigger cities are guarded by soldiers and policemen, armed with sub-machine guns. Now and then, when as we are told by our political masters, there is a 'red alert', even heavy battle tanks make their appearance around the airport's perimeter.

All of us who travel by air, even on holiday, are subject to strict controls. We and our possessions are searched for deadly weapons. To enter the countries of some of our friends and allies we may have to be finger-printed, even strip-searched.

The politicians maintain we need to carry ID cards, as we did in the war six decades since. Our bank accounts are scrutinised, our internet use checked, while satellites monitor our telephone calls, etc. Restrictions and controls, driven by the pathological fear of terrorists, dominate our lives, even those of our children.

Today in the West, our leaders are fighting what they call 'the war against terrorism', as if it was a major armed conflict. They see it not as a clash of great armies, led by conventionally trained commanders, who believe that the destruction of the enemy can only be achieved by victory on the field of battle. Instead it is viewed as a bitter, unrelenting struggle in the shadows, where it is waged against obscure individuals, who could be anybody, a casual acquaintance, a neighbour perhaps, even a friend. The enemy today is basically a loner, armed with a bomb, a sniper's rifle, the grenade-launcher, the car packed with high explosive and driven by some fanatic, perhaps even to lose his own life in the attempt if he can 'take out' the hated enemy.

The more sceptical among us view this alleged 'war against terrorism' with certain reservations. We feel the world is not seething with primeval discontent ready to explode into mindless terrorism. Our great and small cities do not harbour fanatics, mostly made up of other ethnic groups, ready at the drop of a hat to use their weapons of destruction and destroy us.

What kind of world would it be if that were the case? It could lead only to chaos and mass mayhem. Both the 'good' and 'evil', the two categories of morality which now apparently divide our world, would suffer for no good purpose. Mindless terrorism of the kind that our leaders insist flourishes all around us today would be counter-productive, purposeless, achieving nothing.

Things had been different back in the 1940s, when the dying man, who now lay before me on his bed, had introduced his new theory of warfare, which might well entail kidnapping or even the murder of major political figures. No less immoral, Skorzeny and men like him, had attempted by their actions to achieve specific and major aims. Those wartime 'killers' had realised that military power could be broken in the person of one man, especially if that one man was a dictator, such as Hitler, Mussolini, Stalin, or even a 'democratic', elected politician who wielded almost absolute power as did Churchill and Roosevelt.

In the 19th century, the French author Victor Hugo wrote: 'No army can withstand the strength of an idea whose time has come.' The events of World War II prove that he was right. Skorzeny and his kind had shown that. The tales of what they did are not pretty, but in those days sixty years ago, there were few pretty tales. Still our leaders, obsessed by the 'war against terrorism', those global and protracted conflicts with 'insurgents' and the like, might learn a lesson from them.

CHARLES WHITING
SEPTEMBER, 2005

Book One

Murder to Order

'Ye have scarce the soul of a louse,' he said,
'but the roots of sin are there.'

Rudyard Kipling

CHAPTER I

The Truce

'We have not reached the stage in our diplomacy when we have to use assassination as a substitute for diplomacy.'

[Lord Halifax, British Foreign Secretary, spring 1939]

Adolf Hitler believed in *Vorsehung* (providence). The German leader felt that if anything was going to happen to him, such as assassination, there was nothing he could do about it. He had been selected by Fate to achieve something great; he wouldn't die, either by accident or assassination, until he had fulfilled that God-given mission.

Time and time again in the past providence, not planning, had taken care of him. In 1933, for instance, just before he had became master of the Third Reich, he had been involved in a terrible car crash with a truck. He had emerged from the wreckage stating that he couldn't die yet; his mission had not yet been achieved.

It was the same with assassination attempts. Hitler explained that he had many enemies and expected disgruntled Germans and others to try to kill him. But they never would, especially if they came from the German working class. He used to state to his staff quite categorically, *'Mir tut kein deutscher Arbeiter was'* ('no German worker will ever do anything to me'). Once, when he was advised by worried police to use the back entrance to a noisy and angry meeting of workers, Hitler snorted: 'I'm not going through any back door to meet *my* workers!'

As for those aristocratic *Monokelfritzen*,* both civilian and military, who he knew from his Intelligence sources had been trying to eradicate him in these last years of the thirties, he was confident that his personal providence would save him. And in truth, until the very end, providence did protect Hitler from all the attempts on his life, including the 'generals' plot' to kill him in July 1944.

Naturally ever since his election as Imperial Chancellor in 1933, his security guards had taken secret precautions to protect him. Like some

---

*Monocle Fritzes, those high-born, monocled aristocrats Hitler had hated with a passion ever since the Great War.

medieval potentate, all the Führer's food was checked daily before it was served to him. Each day, his personal doctor had to report that the Führer's food supplies were free of poison. Party Secretary Martin Bormann ran daily checks on the water at any place where the Führer might stay to ascertain whether it might contain any toxic substances. Later when Bormann, in his usual fawning manner, started to grow 'bio-vegetables' in his Berchtesgaden gardens for the Führer's consumption,* Hitler's staff wouldn't allow the produce to appear on the master's vegetarian menu.

Once just before the war, a bouquet of roses was thrown into the Führer's open Mercedes. One of his SS adjutants picked it up and a day later started to show the symptoms of poisoning. The roses were examined and found to be impregnated with a poison that could be absorbed through the skin. Thereafter the order was given out secretly that no 'admirer' should be allowed to throw flowers into Hitler's car. In addition, from now on, adjutants would wear gloves.

On another occasion, Hitler, who loved dogs (some said more than human beings), was given a puppy by a supposed admirer. It turned out that the cuddly little dog had been deliberately infected with rabies. Fortunately for Hitler (and not so fortunately for the rest of humanity), the puppy bit a servant before it bit him. It seemed that Hitler's vaunted providence had taken care of him, yet again.

But on this particular Wednesday 8 November 1939, security and his celebrated 'providence' were farthest from Adolf Hitler's mind. The Second World War had been running for two months now. Poland had been conquered within thirty days, while the Anglo-French Coalition had stood by without making the slightest attempt to help their Polish allies. Still the British and French Armies massed on Germany's borders in the west had taken no offensive action. Now Hitler was working on a plan with which he hoped he would convince the Anglo-French appeasers to make peace with Germany and allow him to advance his plans for the Third Reich in Eastern Europe.

Besides, this day he would travel from Berlin to Munich, where the 'Movement' had started. Here he would give his annual speech in the Bavarian capital's *Burgerbraukeller* to the Party faithful: those 'old fighters' who had marched with him back in November 1923 when he had made his first attempt to seize power in the abortive 'Munich Putsch'.

As Hitler prepared himself for his speech, if he did think of the possibility of an attempt on his life, he knew his 'old fighters' would surely

---

*It is not common knowledge that the Nazis started our current craze for growing organic vegetables, free of pesticides, etc. Himmler even set up a 'bio-food' allotment in Dachau concentration camp! The Nazis also introduced cigarette-free zones and health warnings on cigarette packets.

take care of him in Munich. Three years earlier there had been a quarrel between the Munich City Council and the local Chief of Police as to who would protect the Führer during his presence in the *Burgerbraukeller*. In the end the quarrel had become so bitter that both parties had appealed to Hitler himself. The Führer had ruled then: 'At these meetings my "old fighters" will protect me. The responsibility for the Munich Police ends at the door.'

The rule still applied, but Hitler's 'old fighters' had become aged and slack. That November afternoon, as Hitler carried out his personal toilette for the evening, Josef Gerum, a former Munich cop and now a member of the German Army, had been asked almost casually to take over the *Burgerbraukeller*'s security for the duration of the speech. Soon that single ex-cop would be confronted with checking out 3,000 potential suspects: an impossible task.

His mind concentrating on matters other than security, especially how the British might react to his latest proposals for peace, Hitler went through his standard routine of preparing for an important speech. First came the gargle with glycerine and warm water which seemed to give his voice that familiar rasping timbre. Next came the injection. Because of his vegetarian diet and the sixty-odd pills he took a day, 'uppers' and 'downers' and the laxatives that kept him slim, Hitler was plagued by what his doctors called 'meteorism': the need to fart constantly. The injection was to prevent stomach cramps and the need to break wind. Even Hitler, oblivious to his surroundings as he usually was, realised it would be dreadful if he farted at some significant point in his *Burgerbrau* speech.

Then came the problem of sweat. Usually he was soaked in perspiration at the end of one of his two-hour speeches and had to be given anti-cold tablets, washed down with herbal tea and plenty of *Kognak*. So his valet, Linge, a full colonel in the SS, who concealed a pistol beneath his black uniform as most of Hitler's immediate staff did, dressed his master in fresh silk underclothing, at the same time assuring him that the *Burgerbrau* administration had telephoned to say that the temperature would not rise above 12° during the course of the speech.

All that remained for Hitler now was to brief his 'Court Photographer', Professor Heinrich Hoffmann, who had introduced Hitler to his current mistress, Eva Braun. By now Hoffmann knew all Hitler's wishes: the Führer should never be photographed wearing his spectacles or together with any known 'deviant' (and there had been many of those in the early days of the Party). This day, however, the undersized 'Court Photographer' wanted Hitler's instructions on how he should 'shoot' the rostrum party. Hitler insisted that the old 'blood flag' of the '23 Putsch must not be overlooked. Carried by Party Comrade Gimminger, a weedy-looking individual who sported a moustache in the Hitler fashion, the flag must be shown. It was agreed that Hoffmann should combine the two – Hitler and that sacred banner stained with the blood of those who had died back in the beginning. The 'Blood Flag' had to be given prominence.

The hall was packed. Three thousand 'old fighters', including Party *Prominenz* and big-bosomed waitresses in Bavarian costume who could carry ten litres of beers in steins at one time, were jammed together at scrubbed wooden tables, drinking ever more and more Munich beer. Dressed in their brown SA uniform, the pot-bellied veterans were going to make the most of this night when once a year they could feel important again.

Just after eight, the brass band burst into Hitler's favourite march, the *Badenweiler*: all the blare of brass and the thump-thump of the big drum. There was the sudden shuffle of steel-shod, highly polished boots as the expectant veterans rose to their feet, eyes turned towards the door. The Führer was coming!

As agile and vital as he had been back in 1923, Party Commander Gimminger, carrying the 'blood flag', came goose-stepping down the corridor formed by the veterans. A burst of applause. Next moment it was stifled as Hitler himself appeared, striding towards the rostrum a few metres behind Gimminger and his precious flag. Now Hoffmann started to work his Leica. Hitler's smile vanished. His powdered face grew grim. The 'poison dwarf',* the Minister of Propaganda and Public Enlightenment Dr Goebbels, rapped out the '*Sieg Heil*'. A thousand throats echoed the greeting. Hitler flipped up his right hand in acknowledgement and then waited, arms crossed, for silence. The cheering died away.

'*Kameraden, Parteigenossen, Freunde*' ('comrades, party members, friends'), Hitler began his speech with his usual formula. He kept his voice low. It was the old trick. He made his audience listen more intensely this way. It always worked, even with a load of drunks as most of his listeners this evening were.

Clicking away with his camera, Hoffmann thought, as he remarked afterwards: 'Hitler was nervous about something – that was obvious. His speech was much shorter than usual ... some feelings of haste and urgency seemed to be impelling him forward.'

But what the Führer had to say was serious enough. He warned his audience to be prepared for more battle. He attacked the British, especially 'Mister Schurchill', as he called the current First Lord of the Admiralty. He was the one who wanted war not he, Adolf Hitler. He said he wanted nothing from the Western Democracies, save those of the German colonies, 'wrenched from us under false pretences'; Hitler meant the Versailles Treaty of 1919.

As the London *Evening Standard* reported the following day, Hitler

---

*So called on account of his size and vitriolic tongue.

implied he would attack England and 'one cannot count on his *always* telling lies'. In truth Hitler was merely threatening a country which he believed would still reach an agreement with Germany. Perhaps the threat would force the hand of the appeasers and their representatives currently negotiating secretly with those of Nazi Germany.

Shortly after nine o'clock that Wednesday night, Hitler ended his speech, nearly an hour earlier than anticipated. The Party faithful were disappointed. Their great day had been spoiled somehow. Hoffmann, about to leave the beer cellar himself, noted that there were glum faces everywhere at Hitler's early departure. 'The old guard watched with disappointment as Hitler turned abruptly and swiftly left the hall.'

Why he had done so, most of those present had no idea. But his travel plans had changed. Hitler had intended to fly back to Berlin on the following morning. His chief pilot, Hans Baur, however had warned there might be early morning fog. Instead the Führer now had to catch the 9.10 express from Munich's Hauptbahnhof and he didn't want to miss his connection.

But there was something else that made him leave so hastily. Later he told his staff, trying to explain that rapid departure: 'I had a most extraordinary feeling and I don't know how or why – *but I felt compelled to leave the cellar as quickly as I could.*'

About quarter to nine that Wednesday night, two German customs guards were lounging, rifles slung over their shoulders, in the blacked-out darkness of a garden in the border town of Konstanz on the lake of that same name. Through the open window of the local reformatory they listened to the hoarse voice of the Führer transmitted from the Munich *Burgerbraukeller* about a hundred miles away. Like all good Germans, it was their duty to listen to the Führer whenever they had the opportunity to do so*

Now instead of carrying out their routine duties along a stretch of ground that separated Germany from neutral Switzerland, a blaze of lights only metres away, on the lookout for deserters from the Wehrmacht, Jewish fugitives, smugglers trying to cross into Switzerland, they listened to Hitler and his attack on England.

It was just about the time when Hitler started to rant about 'Mister Schurchill' that one of the middle-aged border police (they were now all members of the SS) noticed that there was someone else in the blacked-out garden. Some ten or so metres away, a small figure in civilian clothes was listening intently to the Hitler speech as well. He nudged his companion

---

*When Hitler spoke, the radios had to be turned up in all places of public entertainment and those present were supposed to remain quiet and attentive while he did so.

and the two policemen unslung their carbines. '*Hallo, Sie da*?' one of them cried, '*Was machen Sie*?' ... and then as the figure moved, '*Stehenbleiben oder ich schiesse*'.

But the little civilian made no attempt to run for it. Obediently he raised his hands and waited for the border policemen to approach. Later they said, it was 'almost as if he wanted to be arrested'.

Minutes later their captive was standing in the weak yellow light of the customs post at Kreuzlinger Tor,* the pockets ripped out of his new but cheap suit. Before him on the bare board table, his pathetic few possessions were spread out for inspection. Not that the slightly bored officials thought them very interesting. There was an identity card indicating that their prisoner was one Georg Elser, by trade a carpenter. With it there was a piece of gnawed salami, a badge of the *Rote Frontkaempferbund* (the illegal communist WWI war veterans' association), a bundle of official notices on the manufacture of ammunition, and a picture of the *Burgerbraukeller*, where the Führer had just finished speaking. There were also several pieces of metal, which puzzled one of the policemen. So he asked Elser what he used the metal pieces for. Elser replied in his thick Swabian accent that he needed them for his hobby (a traditional one in Swabia) of clock-making.

One of the officials present who had served in the Army snorted, 'You can't make a clock with those. They're used for making detonators'. That made the desk sergeant look up sharply: 'What in three devils' name would the prisoner be doing with a time detonator?'

Neither the prisoner nor his captors could answer that question. In the end the matter was dismissed as yet another of those myriad meaningless incidents which happened daily on this frontier with Switzerland. Thus it was that at ten o'clock that Wednesday night, Georg Elser was handed over to another official to be taken back to the main German customs post at the lake's biggest town, Konstanz. The charge against the prisoner was not very serious. It was a routine one. He was charged with an attempt to cross into Switzerland illegally. It was that sort of thing that happened on Lake Constance, bordered by three countries – Germany, the former Austria now the Nazi 'Ostmark' and Switzerland, virtually every other day.

Twenty minutes after Elser's departure under arrest, everything changed dramatically, and that humble Swabian carpenter would become an important figure, who would occupy the attention of the Führer, the whole German and SS police *apparat*, even, indirectly, the British Secret service. Suddenly the *Burgerbraukeller* was racked and shaken by a tremendous explosion. As eyewitnesses recounted later, there was 'a

*The post is still there not far from the fence the Swiss built at the time to keep out escapees from Germany, in line with German wishes. At that time, with Germany seemingly all-powerful, the supposedly neutral Swiss cooperated wholeheartedly with their neighbours.

blinding flash of light'. Then the lights flickered and went out. The great pillar behind the rostrum where Hitler had spoken only half an hour or so before 'disappeared in an instant'. Panic broke out. There were screams and shrieks on all sides.

Although the great mass of *Prominenz* and 'old fighters' had left once the Führer had departed, there had been a goodly number who had remained behind to discuss the speech and drink more beer. Of these six 'old fighters' had been killed instantly, along with one of the buxom waitresses, while sixty-three men and women had been injured by the explosion, some of them seriously. Within minutes the 'historic' beer cellar which had seen the birth of Adolf Hitler's rise to power had been transformed into a blood bath.

In those terrible moments as the dying and wounded screamed in panic for help, those who had escaped streamed outside into the blackout, forcing their way through one of the place's four doors, yelling '*A bomb . . . a bomb has exploded in there . . .*'

Just before ten o'clock, while Elser was moved by van to Konstanz (the prisoner seeming so dazed and harmless that the official accompanying him forgot to cuff him), Hitler's train was stopped at Nuremberg, the home of the annual National Socialist rallies. Here Gauleiter Adolf Wagner told the Führer what had just happened in Munich. A suddenly enraged Hitler order 'the criminal' should be apprehended 'at once'. Listening to Hitler and Wagner, local Police Chief Martin realised by the familiar look on the Führer's face that he would soon go into one of his terrible, frightening rages. Martin was right. Hitler ranted, red-faced with fury, that the attack was 'the work of foreign agents . . . probably working for the English'.

While Hitler raged, Heinrich Himmler, the head of the SS, got to work. He had the owner and the whole staff of the *Burgerbraukeller* arrested. A reward of three quarters of a million Reichsmarks was offered for information leading to the arrest of the would-be assassin. If this information came from abroad (again this pointed to the German suspicion that the British were behind the attempt to kill the Führer) there would be an additional 300,000 RM in any foreign currency the informant desired for it.

By this time, Himmler had heard the English were suspected of being the culprits, in particular the London-based Secret Intelligence Service. He decided he would do something to prove the Führer's theory. Did the Führer approve? In the small hours of Thursday 10 November Hitler said he did. Immediately Himmler set about setting the trap, which would show the British up for what they were: a bunch of ruthless killers who would stop at nothing to achieve their nefarious objectives.

Although Britain had been at war with Germany for two months or more, the representatives of the two enemy nations had been carrying on secret talks in neutral Holland for several weeks. The full details of what those talks entailed are still kept secret and will not be revealed until 2015. The official line was – and is – that agents of the SIS in The Hague were talking to German dissidents, military and civilian, who intended to overthrow Hitler and sue for peace with the Western Allies. It seems more likely however that the SIS was working on behalf of those appeasers in Chamberlain's government who wanted an end to the war and were prepared to go to extraordinary lengths, even betrayal of Britain's most sacred promises, in order to achieve that aim. In essence, whatever did transpire was worthwhile. For the 'German dissidents' were really from the SS under the command of Himmler's cunning young ex-lawyer aide, General Walter Schellenberg, who was head of the SS's secret service, the Sicherheitsdienst.

Now in the first hours of 10 November, the telephone began to ring insistently in Schellenberg's hotel bedroom in the Rhenish town of Dusseldorf. The night before the scarfaced general in his late 30s had taken a sleeping pill, but the phone awoke him all the same. He picked up the receiver and heard a deep, rather excited voice. 'What did you say?' it asked.

'Nothing so far,' Schellenberg answered grumpily. 'Who am I speaking to?'

The reply came back sharply, 'This is Reichsführer SS Heinrich Himmler . . . Are you there at last?'

Schellenberg woke up fast. 'Yessir.'

'Well, listen carefully. Do you know what has happened?'

Schellenberg said he didn't.

'Well this evening,' Himmler explained, 'just after the Führer's speech in the beer cellar, someone tried to assassinate him.' Schellenberg noted the sense of outrage in Himmler's voice that anyone should dare to commit such a heinous crime.

'A bomb went off,' Himmler continued. 'There's no doubt that the British Secret Service is behind it all. The Führer and I were already on the train to Berlin when we got the news. He now says – and *this is an order* – when you meet the British agents for your conference, you are to arrest them immediately and bring them to Germany.'

Schellenberg, who would be working for the SIS himself in six years' time, wanted to protest, but an enraged Himmler beat him to it. 'This may mean a violation of the Dutch frontier, but the Führer says that is of no consequence. The SS detachment has already been detailed . . . to help you carry out your mission. So, do you understand everything?'

Again Schellenberg tried to protest, 'Yes Reichsführer but . . .'

'There are no buts,' Himmler interrupted him harshly. 'Do you understand?'

Tamely his subordinate answered, '*Jawohl* Reichsführer.'

The phone went dead.

It was twenty to four in the morning, but Schellenberg knew he couldn't go back to sleep. There was too much planning to do now. He called his subordinate Alfred Naujocks over the hotel's internal line and ordered the big bruiser, who two months before had had the dubious honour of helping to bring Germany into the war,* down to his room.

Sitting in scarlet silk pyjamas and smoking a hand-rolled cigarette from a gold cigarette case, Schellenberg told the burly intellectual thug (Naujocks had once been a right-wing student leader at the University of Kiel) what had happened at Munich that night. He then explained that he and his SS support group, including Naujocks, would have to kidnap the two SS representatives of the British Government at the Dutch border town of Venlo. 'Frankly,' Schellenberg added, 'I hate the idea . . . To kidnap two of their best Secret Service men in broad daylight is a bit dangerous to say the least. But it's an order from Himmler – and that means Hitler. So we'd better start thinking about it.'

In the end the plan they worked out consisted of meeting the two SIS agents, Payne and Best, at the little border post's Cafe Backus. Disguised as German officers in mufti, Schellenberg and a fellow plotter would lure the British into a false sense of security. Thereupon, Naujocks and his fellow thugs would come racing through the nearby German frontier post in their Mercedes, firing at the Dutch border guards if they resisted, snatch Payne and Best and bundle them across the frontier into the Reich.

Like Schellenberg, Naujocks didn't care for the idea one bit. He had been involved in this kind of nasty business before. Then there was the problem of Schellenberg himself. As Naujocks recalled later (the big thug also went over to the British and the SIS in 1944):

> There was no doubt that he [Schellenberg] was a clever diplomat, a master of deception, a man with a brilliant mind . . . But with all his airs and graces [he] wouldn't be much help when you found yourself at the wrong end of a Luger.

So Naujocks suggested to his boss that he, Schellenberg, should take no part in the actual kidnapping; that should be left entirely to himself and his experienced SS operatives. All that Schellenberg needed to do was to go inside the cafe and order a drink. When he saw Best's big American car approach, he was to go outside as if to greet them. That would be the signal for Naujocks' Mercedes. The driver would cut across the border at

---

*Naujocks had played a large role in 'Operation Canned Goods', the faked, supposedly Polish attack on the German radio transmitter at the border town of Gleiwitz. The attack had been used as an excuse by Hitler for marching into Poland on 31 August 1939.

top speed and in this manner surprise the Dutch guards. Before they could recover and start firing, Best and Payne, the two SIS agents, would be Naujocks' prisoners and on their way to the Reich and whatever kind of unpleasant fate awaited them there.

Schellenberg, who had a great respect for the sanctity of his own hide, agreed readily to Naujocks' suggestion. This day, then, they would kidnap the two middle-aged Englishmen, whom Schellenberg had supposedly fooled into believing that he was a representative of the Wehrmacht's* resistance to Hitler, and use them to reveal to the world that the dastardly British had actually plotted to kill the Führer in Munich. It would show, as the 'poison dwarf,' Minister of Propaganda Dr Goebbels would soon maintain, that once again the 'English Secret Service' had employed 'its time-honoured method of assassination'. It was the same one that 'perfidious Albion' had used in the past to eradicate its opponents such as 'Tsar Nicholas II, Archduke Franz Ferdinand, T E Lawrence, King Alexander of Yugoslavia and the Frenchman Louis Barthou.

The German Geheime Staatspolizei (the Gestapo) had been using torture ever since it had been taken over by the Nazis in 1933. Naturally torture wasn't anything particularly new in continental European countries. All European police forces in the early thirties had employed kicks, punches and physical threats to intimidate their prisoners. In many cases they had also used torture. The Italian secret police, the OVRA, for example had routinely employed water tortures and massive doses of castor oil, with unpleasant digestive results, on Mussolini's political prisoners; while their Austrian neighbours had made use of whips and so-called 'warm cells', in which the heating was turned up so high that the unfortunate victim thought he was going to be roasted to death.

But none of these European police forces (and that included Stalin's hated 'green caps', the NKVD) had systematised and refined their methods to the same degree as that achieved by the Gestapo. With unimportant prisoners, the Gestapo Kommissare limited themselves usually to kicks and blows. Perhaps they might make the unfortunate individual clean the floor with a toothbrush or the 'shit bucket' with his bare hands; or even urinate on the prisoner to show him just how powerful they were.

Important prisoners or those refusing to reveal key information were treated very differently. A whole bureaucratic system, rising in intensity, had been worked out for such prisoners. They could have their toenails or

---

*It must be pointed out that the main eyewitnesses that Thursday 9 November 1939 were all under pressure from the SIS when they gave their accounts after the war of what had happened at Venlo. Payne and Best were in disgrace, whereas the two Germans, Naujocks and Schellenberg, who could well have been accused of war crimes, were very dependent on the British.

teeth pulled out one by one. There was the water torture when the prisoner was ducked in a bath of cold water time and time again until the unfortunate thought he was going to choke to death. There was the 'bucket torture', in which the prisoner had an enamel pail placed over his head. The pail was then struck repeatedly with a broomstick until he bled from nose and ears and felt he was going mad with the noise.

There were other, more sexually perverted means of torture – the vice which crushed a man's testicles, the electrodes that could be attached to a female prisoner's nipples and vagina, etc. But what made the Gestapo's methods of torture different from those of other continental countries was that a record had to be kept of each session, which was usually conducted in the presence of a prison doctor; and that each degree of punishment had to be ordered by a senior officer and a duplicate record kept. There was no place in the German system for the whims of some sadistic bully. Here everything had to be carried out with *deutsche Grundlichkeit und Ordnung* (German thoroughness and order).

In the case of the two kidnapped British SIS officers, Best and Payne, their interrogation was to be carried out under the orders of three of the most feared men in the Third Reich. First there was Heinrich Himmler, head of the SS. After him came Reinhard Heydrich, his deputy in effect, of whom it was said that even Hitler was afraid of the SS General he called 'the man with the iron heart.* But the man who would actually carry out the interrogations, the third of the group, had a nickname that was supposed to strike the fear of death in any prisoner he interrogated, General of the SS 'Gestapo' Mueller.

Best, the older of the two Britons, was brought from Holland to Gestapo Headquarters at 10 Prinz Albrechtstrasse, Berlin, hooded, handcuffed and with his feet strapped together. He knew this was standard Gestapo operating procedure and it didn't worry him particularly. He knew too that he must expect blows, threats and eventually torture and this *did* worry him. For he felt he knew a great deal about the SIS operations in Europe and wondered how long he could keep this information secret once the Gestapo thugs started to work him over. What Best did not know was that the Gestapo was not particularly interested in his spy missions inside the Reich, but in the supposed British connected with the attempted assassination of the Führer.

The Briton was confronted by 'Gestapo' Mueller almost immediately. He found the German to be a 'dapper, exceptionally good-looking man, dressed in a grey uniform jacket, black riding breeches and top boots'.

Mueller, once a Bavarian secret policeman, who before 1933 had chased Nazis with the same relentlessness he employed against communists, bellowed at Best in best Gestapo fashion:

*We shall hear more of Heydrich later.

You are in the hands of the Gestapo! Don't imagine that we shall show you the slightest consideration! The Führer has already shown the world that he is invincible and soon he will come and liberate the people of England from Jews and Plutocrats such as you. You are in the greatest danger and if you want to live another day you must be careful.

Mueller was behaving just as Best expected he would: a jumped up member of the working classes, now enjoying the rank of general and the trappings that went with it. What Best didn't know then was that Mueller was the only professional policeman in the place. In addition, the young former mechanic had won two decorations for bravery in WWI and as a lowly sergeant pilot had set off in 1918 on a lone mission to bomb Paris. 'Gestapo' Mueller, in spite of his bluster, was not a man to be underestimated.

For a while the SS general continued to shout and bluster. He bellowed:

You don't seem to realise your position. It is war. You are no longer an honoured guest in Germany. [Prior to the war Best had often been to the Reich as a supposed wealthy British businessman.] You are a helpless prisoner of the Gestapo. Don't you know where you are? At the headquarters of the Gestapo. We can do anything we like with you, *anything* . . .

But for the time being Best was safe, for as we shall see, the Gestapo bigshots were now fully occupied with the humble little Swabian carpenter Georg Elser. In the second week of his imprisonment, however, they led him into another room and came to attention in front of a tall, blond, arrogant-looking, youngish SS general, who was obviously Mueller's superior. Best didn't know it at the time, but he was now being confronted by the individual Hitler called 'the man with the iron heart'. It was Reinhard Heydrich, an officer feared not only by opponents of the Nazi regime, but even by his own high-ranking officers, including 'Gestapo' Mueller.

Heydrich started threatening Best immediately. Lounging against the side of the table, dangling his long legs, the expert violinist and German fencing champion shouted:

So far you have been treated like an officer and gentleman, but don't think this will go on if you don't behave better than you have done. You have two hours left to confess everything. If you don't I shall hand you over to the Gestapo, who are used to dealing with such gangsters and criminals. You won't enjoy their methods one bit.

14

According to his own post-war account, Best turned to Mueller and asked: 'Who is this excitable young man?'

At this Heydrich 'really went off the deep end and literally foamed at the mouth; at all events he sprayed me most liberally with his saliva.'

Swiftly a somewhat shocked Mueller ushered his boss out of the room. Later the Gestapo chief came back and assured Best: '*Die Suppe wird nie so heiss gegessen wie gekocht.*' ('The soup is never eaten as hot as it is cooked' – an old German saying meaning things are never as bad as they seem.)

So, if we are to believe the disgraced Best's post-war account, he had confronted and overawed the three most powerful men (after Himmler) in the German police state: Schellenberg, Mueller and Heydrich. But in essence these Germans were no longer particularly interested in what Best had to reveal of SIS operations in Europe. For he had spilled the beans, as he revealed Stevens, who had done the same. In a note smuggled to Best at Sachsenhausen Concentration Camp in June 1940, Stevens wrote that he had 'been compelled to tell the truth. Any other line would have been useless. They already knew too much. I was told if I did not talk, I'd soon be made to.'

But by now the two British SIS men had been relegated to the status of mere witnesses. For Himmler himself had taken up the interrogation of Georg Elser, whom he realised was the real culprit. The simple left-wing carpenter had been the one who had planted the bomb in a pillar behind the rostrum in the *Burgerbraukeller*. From August 1939 onwards, he had secreted himself in the beer hall after closing hours virtually every night and dug his way into the pillar. Finally he had made a hole sufficiently large to conceal the explosives he had stolen from a quarry where he had once worked and sealed them up with a primitive timing device set to go off when Hitler was speaking. As he confessed to Himmler, [in this way] 'I could get rid of the leadership' and prevent another world war like the one he had fought in in 1918.

Naturally Himmler could not use the full story which Elser had confessed to him after, incidentally, being tortured. Hitler would never buy the idea that an ordinary German worker, even a 'Red', had tried to kill him. He had make more out of Elser's confession. Thus it was that on Tuesday 21 November Himmler announced that he had apprehended the man who had planted the bomb in Munich which had narrowly missed killing the Führer. He was Georg Elser, aged 36. Behind him was Otto Strasser, a former Nazi big shot, who had fled Germany after Hitler had had his brother shot in 1934. Now Strasser was a bitter enemy of the Führer, spreading horrible tales, among other things, about Hitler's perverted sex life. At the same time Himmler revealed that a 'certain Mr Best' and his accomplice 'a certain Captain Stevens' had been taken by the Gestapo across the Dutch-German border ten days earlier on 9 November 1939.

As the American correspondent William Shirer noted in his diary that Tuesday:

> What Himmler and his gang are up to, obviously, is to convince the gullible German people that the British government tried to win the war by murdering Hitler and his chief aides.

Indeed, according to that scenario, Himmler and Schellenberg were now developing for the great show trial to come. Elser had long been in contact with Strasser in Switzerland – why else had he been found on the Swiss border on the night of his arrest? He had been the courier between the Reich and that neutral country.

In December '38, Elser had met Strasser at the Hotel Bauer du Lac in Zurich. Here Strasser had introduced him to some 'British gentlemen'. Later Strasser had told the country carpenter that he was now working for the British. He added that the British were determined to get rid of Hitler and that the 'Tommies' stood more chance of doing so than he, Strasser, alone and relatively powerless in Switzerland. From now on, Strasser informed Elser, he'd take his orders from the British, in particular from Herr Best. The latter lived in Holland and arrangements would be made for Elser to meet him there. As a token of British goodwill, Elser was then handed a thousand Swiss francs. In other words, as Himmler and Schellenberg developed the scenario for the show trial *à la Russe*,* Elser was to be portrayed not as an honest if simple-minded German worker, but as a bought man in the pay of the future enemy, the British.

Over the next months, according to Himmler, Elser had betrayed to the British secret information about Germany's war industry (for a time he had worked in a shell factory). In October 1939 Elser had met Captain Best (now the enemy as Germany was at war with Britain) at Venlo on the Dutch border. There he was given instructions on how to plant a bomb in the Munich beer cellar. At Venlo he was promised a fortune, namely 40,000 Swiss francs, for a successful job.

At first the carpenter refused. After all he was a German citizen. Best had put pressure on him. He had threatened the other man that he would be denounced to the Gestapo as a British spy if he didn't carry out their instructions. Elser gave in. Thereupon he was given an address in Germany, where he would receive further instructions and the bomb. This then was the scenario that Himmler ordered Elser to learn. Soon the carpenter would be confronted with Best personally and would identify him as the man behind the dastardly plot to kill the Führer.

---

*At this time there was a series of show trials in Russia showing that Russians, even of the highest rank, had been in the pay of the enemies of the State and had been prepared even to kill the 'Little Father'– Stalin.

But things weren't going as Himmler had planned. The foreign press was getting impatient. Each day at the briefings in Goebbels' Ministry of Propaganda, the German press spokesman was greeted by a chorus of when will Elser be tried?', which, as Shirer noted, 'always provoked scarcely restrained laughter from the correspondents'. Goebbels lost his nerve. The 'poison dwarf', who always maintained that 'if you're going to tell a lie, tell a *big* one', announced on 22 November that Best and Stevens had organised a murder plot against the Führer. They were under arrest now. In due course they would be brought to trial. Goebbels went on to cry in that high-pitched Rhenish voice of his that the plot was 'typical of the English Secret Service's time honoured method of assassination'.

But already Himmler's faith in a show trial was beginning to weaken. He staged a meeting between Best and his supposed subordinate Elser. The latter was brought to Prinz Albrechtstrasse in chains, where he was made to sit on a bench on the upper floor where important Gestapo prisoners were interrogated. He was ordered to remain perfectly still and observe everyone who went by in the next few minutes on their way to the latrines which were located just beyond the bench. One of them would be an Englishman and he was very important.

Elser waited for five minutes until a tall, dark man appeared. He was heading for the latrines. Elser did as was expected of him. Then he watched the tall, dark man again as he returned from the earthen privy.

Thereafter Elser was taken in his chains to an office where Schellenberg and Heydrich were waiting for him. The former now told the prisoner his life was forfeit. He had become a *Todeskandidat* (a death candidate). The only way he might save his life was to do exactly what he was told. He had just seen a certain English Secret Service agent, named Captain Best. Soon Best would be placed on trial, accused of the most heinous crimes, and he, Elser, would appear at that trial as a witness for the prosecution. It was the only way he could save himself. Did he understand?

He did.

'Good,' Schellenberg said and began his briefing, 'Back in December 1938 . . . in Switzerland . . .'

But the steam was going out of the trumped-up charges. Elser, who was proving to be slightly soft in the head, didn't look at all the sort of person who would be picked by the infamous English Secret Service to play a major part in a plot to eradicate the Führer. Even Hitler himself wouldn't believe that of the humble Swabian carpenter. The foreign press thought the same. As Shirer noted in his diary that month: 'The censor cut out all references in my script [Shirer broadcast regularly to the States, one of the first correspondents to do so] to the Reichstag fire.' By this the portly, bespectacled American meant the Nazis' show trial of the half-mad Dutchman van der Lubbe, who was accused of setting fire to the Berlin Reichstag building back in 1933. That had been a set-up and Shirer believed, as did many other of the foreign correspondents in the German capital, that any trial of Elser would be the same. A fake.

There were others too, who observed that *if* there had been a plot to kill the Führer, he must have known about it in advance. Why else would he have broken his annual custom of staying behind in the *Burgerbraukeller* to chat a little with his 'old fighters'? Instead he had cut his speech short and departed much earlier. There had been no need to try to catch the express to Berlin on time. After all he was the Führer, the leader of a nation of eighty million people, with boundless power at his command. Hitler didn't wait for trains; trains waited for him.

Nor could Hitler, after some consideration, believe that the redoubtable British Secret Service would pick someone like Elser to carry out its work for them. As he once told his staff: 'The British Secret Service has a great tradition . . . Germany possesses nothing comparable to it. The cunning and perfidy of the British Secret Service is known to the world.' Why didn't his own 'man with the iron heart', Heydrich, the head of the SS's police apparat model himself on what he had read about the 'Secret Service' with his blue pencil and pen, reserved for his own signature on all documents and the red and green lights in front of his office door (for 'do not enter' and 'enter'), as 'C', the head of the British organisation was supposed to?*

In the end, then, the idea of a great show trial was dropped. Himmler, still believing that one day his time would come, kept the three main participants on ice in various concentration camps until he knew that Germany had lost the war and that the time had come to save his own skin. Best and Stevens survived to be returned home to be dismissed by the SIS in disgrace. 'Special Prisoner Elser', as he had been titled throughout the war, was to suffer 'a fatal accident'.

As Himmler wrote to the commandant of the Dachau Concentration Camp in the first week of April 1945:

> During one of the next terror raids on Munich or in the area of Dachau, 'Eller' is to suffer a fatal accident. I request that 'Eller' is to be liquidated as soon as a raid starts, but in a discreet manner. For this reason, only a few persons should know of the matter . . . After receiving this letter and carrying out the operation, I request you destroy this letter.

Four days later, as the air raid sirens started to sound their dread warning, an NCO and an armed prisoner brought 'Special Prisoner Eller'

---

*Back in the early thirties, when Himmler had asked the new recruit Heydrich to draw up a plan for a new SS intelligence organisation, the latter had done so based on the novels about the British Secret Service he had read as an off-duty naval officer.

out of his cell. Moments later the armed prisoner had liquidated' Georg Elser. Now came the turn of the armed prisoner. His rifle was taken from him. He was forced to kneel. The CO, Untersturmführer Stiller, Schellenberg's representative in Dachau (his job was to spy on the camp commandant), thereupon blew the back of the man's head off. Later the two victims disappeared into the ovens, their ashes scattered to the wind.

Back in early 1939, when Elser had conceived the idea of assassinating Hitler, the SIS and the British Foreign Office were approached by the 'Quiet Canadian' and a serving officer in the British Army, Colonel F N Mason-Macfarlane. The 'Quiet Canadian', the industrialist William Stephenson, who was soon to contribute a great deal to Britain's secret war against the Germans, and Mason-Macfarlane, currently British military attache in Berlin, first met the Deputy Chief of the SIS, Colonel Stewart Menzies.

The two would-be plotters explained to the ex-Etonian and former officer in the Life Guards, who had influence at Court, that they had a plan to shoot Hitler. The assassination would be carried out by a skilled marksman from the safety of the British Embassy compound in Berlin. The British Embassy, they maintained, was an ideal location for the attempt. It was located only a few blocks from Hitler's Chancellery and the Führer's motorcade frequently passed close by.

Menzies and his boss, the dying Admiral Sinclair, were cautiously optimistic about the chances of the plan succeeding. But it was a concept totally new to them. The Secret Service did not kill its enemies, well at least not in Western Europe, especially if the intended victim was the head of state of Europe's most powerful country, Germany. The two SIS officers decided it would be wiser to pass on the assassination plan to the British cabinet, in particular, to the 'Holy Fox', Foreign Secretary Lord Halifax.*

The tall, austere politician, who was later considered by historians of the period to belong to that group of industrialists, aristocrats, big businessmen and politicians who wished to appease Hitler, was not pleased with the plan. Like so many of the British ruling class of the time, he saw Russian communism as the main danger to Britain's future and her Empire. Hitler was well-known as being a rabid opponent of Russia. Therefore, if Britain could come to terms with Hitler's Germany and left it basically to do what it liked in Continental Europe, that would be to Britain's great advantage. In due course, Hitler might well direct his well-known territorial ambitions against the Soviet Union. That could result in a war that could probably ruin both Germany and Russia, something which would be to Britain's advantage. In essence it was the

*Thus nicknamed because he was very religious and delighted in fox-hunting, despite his crippled arm.

old British diplomatic tactic of playing one European power off against the other.

Now, although the Prime Minister Mr Chamberlain had turned against Hitler since his meeting with him in Munich the year before – 'the commonest little swine it has ever been my misfortune to meet' – the PM agreed with Halifax that any attempt on Hitler's life should be forbidden. Halifax went even further. He took a moral stand. As Chamberlain agreed that the SIS should make an approach to supposedly anti-Nazi elements in Germany (which, as we have seen, resulted in the Venlo fiasco and the kidnapping of Best and Stevens), Halifax declared, rejecting the Mason-Stephenson assassination plan totally: 'We have not reached the stage in our diplomacy when we have to use assassination as a substitute for diplomacy.'

'The Holy Fox' naturally took the high moral ground as was expected of him. One did not fight a war for democracy, freedom, etc., and at the same time plot to kill the enemy leader. And assassination attempts of that kind set a bad precedent. If the British tried to kill Hitler and it became known that they were the instigators of the assassination attempt, what was to stop the Germans making an attempt on Chamberlain's life, that of the 'King-Emperor' and later that of Winston Churchill?

Besides, it would be argued later, if the British killed Hitler, who might take his place? What would his policies be? Perhaps the possible successor might shy away from tackling the enormous might of the Soviet Union? The man who might follow Hitler could well be more of a pragmatist with a better grip of political realities than Adolf Hitler with his crazy belief in providence and his own divine mission? No, any successful attempt to get rid of Hitler by assassination could be followed by so many imponderables that it wouldn't be worth the risk.

For moral and practical reasons then in 1939, the year WWII broke out, the British government* were not even prepared to consider an attempt on Hitler's life or that of any other major European leader. It just was not the 'done thing'.

Just as the British decided for various reasons not to indulge in political assassination, the German leadership came to the same decision. In the

---

*There were other, unofficial plans, to do away with Hitler, it seems. The London *Daily Telegraph* (22 Nov. 1998) records: 'A daring pre-war plot to assassinate Adolf Hitler using a brilliant RAF pilot on a low-level bombing mission has been discovered. Arthur Clouston was offered £1 million in the spring of 1938 – worth £30 million today – by an unidentified Jewish businessman. Mr Clouston was asked to fly across the North Sea to bomb a military parade being inspected by the Nazi leader. After carrying out the mission he was expected to fly to Sweden, to safety and a new life abroad.' Needless to say, the late Air Commodore Clouston, who won two DSOs in the war, didn't carry out the suicidal mission. He died in 1984 aged 75.

Nazi Party, prior to and after Hitler's takeover of power, it was not uncommon for the Führer and his cronies to kill political opponents. In 1934 Hitler personally instigated the wholesale slaughter of the leadership of the same 'storm troopers' (SA), who under the leadership of Ernst Roehm had helped him to become Chancellor, the so-called Roehm Putsch. After 1933, Hitler's thugs, such as Naujocks and Heydrich, had been instrumental in having German political leaders who had fled abroad liquidated in the same brutal manner.

But Hitler had had only German nationals murdered. He had always stopped short of ordering the death of foreign political leaders, however much he must have hated such men as the Russian dictator Stalin. It is clear from the diaries of two of his most senior espionage chiefs, Canaris and Lahousen, who could have been instrumental in planning any assassination, that the Führer never gave them an order to prepare for such an operation – at least in the first three years of the global conflict.

Although Hitler was quite accustomed to the bloody business of political assassination, as we have seen,* it had apparently never entered his head to have Chamberlain, Churchill, Daladier or any other of the Western leaders done away with. We do not know whether any plan to do so, especially in the case of his pet hate in the Western camp, Winston Churchill, was put to Hitler. If such a plan was proposed by, say Heydrich, Hitler must have vetoed it.

But neither the diary of Admiral Canaris of the Abwehr (back in 1921 he had been involved personally in the murder of the left-wing radical leader Rosa Luxembourg), nor that of his subordinate Colonel Lahousen, responsible for the German Secret Service's 'dirty tricks' department, reveal any such murder plans.

Hitler, it can be concluded, never really contemplated the possibility of murdering his opponents. It seems, too, that although Britain's SIS did consider the assassination of the German leader, the plan was vetoed right at the top. It was as if there was an unspoken truce between Germany and the 1939 wartime Franco-British alliance not to make an attempt on the lives of the enemy's major leaders (soon to include in May 1940 Benito Mussolini of Italy).

In those early years of WWII a certain set of rules of conduct still determined what could and could not be done. After all, this was a period when portly, bespectacled Sir Kingsley Wood, British Minister of Air, erupted angrily in the House of Commons when asked by an MP why the RAF set fire to the German Black Forest with incendiary bombs. He snapped that was impossible. After all, 'the Black Forest was private property'.

*During Hitler's career as right-wing politician from 1921 onwards, there were 376 political assassinations carried out in Germany, mostly against left-wing politicians.

21

But the times were changing. As 1940 and the 'phoney war' gave way to 1941 and the shooting war, the British authorities seemed to have decided it was time to take off the kid gloves. The country stood alone against the might of an all-conquering Germany. Now the Third Reich dominated the whole of Western Europe in an empire bigger than that of the Romans. British arms had been defeated and were continuing to be defeated everywhere on three continents.

In 1940 Winston Churchill, dissatisfied with the tame, old fashioned methods of the pre-war SIS, set up a new and rival secret service, the SOE. His first order to this new organisation gave a signal of what he expected of it and the future. It was 'Set Europe Ablaze!'. Whether that order included plans to assassinate enemy leaders was not made clear at the time. But as General Gubbins, the head of this new SOE, would remark later, what was now going to happen in the war in the shadows would become 'bloodier than the Somme'.

CHAPTER II

The Truce is Broken

'There is nothing more exhilarating than to be shot at without result.'

Winston Churchill

Saturday was always a busy day in the little Shropshire market town of Whitchurch. Even in wartime, with the shops increasingly short of unrationed goods, the locals turned out to see and be seen. Not only the locals, however. On Saturdays the town was normally packed with soldiers, hundreds of them from their camp in the lush parkland belonging to Lord Cholmondeley, some seven miles to the north.

But these were not British soldiers. The small, squat men with broad slav faces, who spoke a kind of fractured English, were Czechs and Slovaks. Originally back in 1939 when Hitler had marched into the western parts of their country, they had been in the Czech Army. Then a goodly number of them, especially the regulars, had fled to France to become a second 'Czech Legion'.* After the defeat of France in the summer of 1940, they had fled again – this time to Britain, the only country now engaged in fighting the Nazis.

They hadn't been happy soldiers, so far away from their home country. In fact some of them had mutinied under the leadership of pro-communist elements.**

The British, who had hushed the matter up, had segregated the pro-communist elements and posted most of them to the Pioneer Corps as part of the British Army. Now, however, those who had not been hived off to the British 'pick and shovel brigade' prepared to fight the Germans when the time came.

This particular Saturday afternoon in the April of 1941, however,

---

*The first Czech Legion had been a prominent anti-Bolshevik force during the Russian civil war of 1918/20.
**One of them had been a teenage private, named Hoch, who would later become Private Gerald du Maurier (after the popular cigarette of the time) and finally Captain Robert Maxwell, the notorious 'Captain Bob' of the post-war years.

thoughts of combat were far from the minds of these young foreign soldiers. Like soldiers the world over, when they were off duty, they were after beer and women, preferably in that order. But this was England and in this funny country with its strange laws about drinking, the 'pubs' (all the Czech soldiers knew that word of English at least) were still closed, so the Czechs concentrated on the women.

Thus it was that two teenage sisters, Edna and Lorna Ellison from the neighbouring village of Ightfield, found themselves being followed by two of the squat foreign soldiers. Torn between curiosity and propriety, the two sisters chanced a glance behind them. They saw two young Czech NCOs, well turned-out with pressed uniforms and highly polished boots. Both were perhaps ten years older than they were. Still they were foreigners and soldiers and their 'mum' had warned the girls against such types. So they hurried to the bus stop to wait for their bus home.

But before they could leave, the two Czechs caught up with them. One searched in the pocket of his battledress until he found a scrap of paper. Laboriously the soldier scribbled a few words on it with a stub of pencil and then pushed the note through a narrow gap in the bus window. 'Please meet here tomorrow,' it read. Then the old country bus was drawing away and the two young girls started to chatter excitedly between themselves. They'd 'clicked', and with two foreign soldiers at that. What were they going to do? Should they tell 'mum'?

They did and so Jan Kubis and Josef Gabchik entered the humdrum life of the Ellison family, which temporarily adopted the Czech soldiers, inviting them to their modest home whenever the two of them were off duty. Occasionally at weekends, when they stayed, Mrs Ellison would take up a tray of tea and toast, spoiling the Czechs after a hard week of training at their camp. One Sunday, she went up with the tray to discover the bedcloths had slipped down from Jan's naked back. Now what she saw made the middle-aged housewife understand why Jan was always so serious. Down the small of his back were the scars of seven swastikas which had been branded there at some time or other.

Mrs Ellison knew little of the two Czechs' past history. But she had heard of the Gestapo and what they had done to those Czechs who had resisted the German occupation of their country. She guessed the scars had something to do with the Germans and now she realised why the two soldiers always carried loaded pistols. They had been captured and perhaps tortured before; they weren't going to let that happen again. That's why they carried the pistols.

Then came that last weekend at the Ellisons' cottage. Somehow the two soldiers had managed to sneak out of their camp to say good-bye. They gave Mrs Ellison and her girls a few little gifts. Then they emptied their pockets of their personal possessions and passed them over to Mrs Ellison, saying to her in their broken English: 'Keep these and we will come back for them.'

At the door, Mrs Ellison kissed the two soldiers goodbye and said, with tears in her eyes: 'Take care of yourselves. We'll look forward to the next time we meet. The war can't go on for ever.'

The soldiers nodded somberly and left. The Ellisons would never see them again. But a few days after they had departed Mrs Ellison found a little note they had left behind. On it was written: 'Remember please your Czech friends, who will never forget the nice time spent with you. Yours sincerely, Jan.'

And that was the last that the Ellisons would ever hear of their two Czech friends in WWII. It was only later that they learned that they had offered their hospitality to two heroes (or assassins) whichever way one looked at the Czechs and what Fate had in store for them, who would change in their own way the history of Central Europe. For now it was September 1941 and the plan was taking shape in London that would ensure that Mrs Ellison would never see her 'two Czech boys' again.

In that first week of September 1941, Reinhard Heydrich telephoned his wife unexpectedly at their home in Berlin's Augustastrasse. Since the Venlo incident back in November 1939, Heydrich had gone from strength to strength. During the intervening period he had expanded the German police apparatus enormously. Not only that, he had taken 'leave' from his police duties to qualify as a pilot and, against Hitler's wishes, had flown combat missions against the new enemy, Soviet Russia. Once he had been shot down behind Russian lines and in a forty-eight-hour trek had made his way back successfully to the German positions. That had earned him another medal for bravery but also the Führer's displeasure that he had risked some of Germany's greatest secrets if he had been captured and tortured by the 'Reds'.

But Heydrich's overweening ambition and fervent desire to further his career had meant he had not seen his big, blonde wife Lina for weeks, even months at a time. Now, as he told his pregnant wife that he had just learned that he was to be posted to a new job of importance in Occupied Czechoslovakia, Lina burst into tears. The North German schoolteacher's daughter, who had first met Heydrich when she had fallen out of her canoe and he had dived into the sea to rescue her, sobbed, 'I'll never see you again.'

The passion that Heydrich always tried to conceal as being unGerman burst through, 'Oh now, 'he protested.' It's my big chance. Up to now my career has been negative. Now I'm going to do something positive. I'm sick of getting rid of people . . . putting them behind bars. This is my chance to do something with purpose.'

That 'something' was as the new Reich Protector of Bohemia and Moravia, the key centres of Czech industrial production, which as soon as

Heydrich had completed his 'reforms' would be turning out a quarter of all Germany's light armoured vehicles.*

Three days after his arrival in Prague on 2 October 1941, Heydrich summoned the German leaders of the occupied country to his HQ. He assured them that the Czechs had no role to play in the future of Germany's 'New Europe'. 'The racially valuable part of the Czech race could be Germanised,' he announced, whereas the rest would be 'sterilised or placed against the wall'. However, as he made clear, he had radical, short-term plans for the Czechs. These consisted of '*Zuckerbrot und Peitsche*' (a carrot and a big stick). Any Czech worker-opposition to the Germans, inspired by the Russians, who were now using members of the former Czech communist party to sabotage war production, would be overcome by bribes and, if necessary, 'liquidation' of the anti-German elements.

Within a week of his arrival in Prague, the energetic ex-policeman (as he now thought of himself) was putting his plan into action. While his Gestapo dealt with the Czech dissidents (it was then that he reputedly gained the nickname, the 'Butcher of Prague'), Heydrich was busy bribing the Czech workers into obedience and naturally increased war production. Fat rations were increased for heavy workers. He stopped the black market in cigarettes so that the workers could obtain more 'lung torpedoes', as Heydrich called them. Hotels were requisitioned for Czechs so that they could go for a '*Kur*' in the German fashion. For the first time since the foundation of the Czech Republic after WWI, Czech workers were granted a comprehensive sickness insurance and social security scheme on the German model.

The results were immediate. Despite the protests of the illegal Czech communists, the workers began to co-operate. Production of heavy armament and, in particular armoured vehicles, started to rise to make up the losses incurred by the Wehrmacht in Russia. The great mass of the Czechs, devoid of leaders who had either fled, were dead or behind bars, tamely accepted the dictates of the new Protector.

Back in London, the Czech Government in Exile viewed the developments in their homeland with alarm. They had been in England for nearly three years and had little real contact with their native country. There the two main forces were the German occupiers and the Czech underground communist party. As for the Czech right-wing resistance which supported the exiled President, Eduard Benes, it had been virtually wiped out by Heydrich and his German predecessors.

In general, Benes that year was in a difficult position. There was a Czech

---

*It is an irony of WWII that when the Allies landed in Europe in June '44, many of the war weapons employed against them were Skoda cannon and Renault light tanks and self-propelled guns.

Army in exile, but it wasn't fighting, and indeed the only Czechs in England actively engaged in combatting the Germans were those fighting with the RAF. Haunted by Munich, Benes must have wondered, if the war ended in Britain's favour and that of her new ally, Soviet Russia, whether his homeland might be sacrificed again by the British. Just as Britain had stood by and allowed Czechoslovakia to be swallowed up by Germany before WWII, would the same thing happen again with the British conceding that his homeland was in a victorious Russia's sphere of influence?

Thus it was, when this most delicate matter of Benes' presidency as head of the Czech Government in Exile in London was raised that autumn, plus all its accompanying dangers for the Czech people, Benes must have felt that he had no viable alternative but to go along with the startling proposal that was being put forward secretly in the British capital.

It was that Heydrich, now no longer a mere policeman, but the head of an occupied state, should be assassinated. The aim, it seemed, was that this assassination should be not only a warning to the other senior Germans running Benes' occupied homeland, but also to those Czechs who were collaborating with the enemy.

But any assassination of a senior German official, such as the murder of Heydrich, would, Benes realised right from the start, bring down the wrath of the occupiers on the occupied. How did Benes or anyone else involved in the plot square that with their conscience? Kill Heydrich and the Germans would carry out massive reprisals. Already in occupied Russia the Germans had wiped out whole villages, where there had been the murder of German military and civilians. Over the last year or so since the Germans had invaded Soviet Russia, their conduct there had become increasingly savage and barbaric.

We do not know how Benes faced up to this problem of reprisals. We do know, however, that he understood he couldn't be seen back in his homeland as the cause of whatever mass retaliation the Germans undertook if Heydrich was assassinated. The plan to kill the German 'Protector' had to be kept very secret. As a result none of the Czech ministers in exile were consulted. Nothing, as far as is known, was put down on paper. All communications were oral. Right from the start Benes, bearing that terrible knowledge of what would happen once Heydrich was eliminated, was determined nothing should be traced back to him. In the end, as far as the Czechs who would carry out the murder were concerned, the plan was limited to President Benes himself and a few Intelligence officers under the command of the Head of Czech Intelligence, Colonel (later General) Frantisek Moravec, an old hand in the spying game.

However, the Czech Government in Exile could do nothing of any importance without British approval. The British were the paymasters;

they paid for everything, from the bully beef consumed by the Czech troops to the quality flats their leaders enjoyed renting in the more fashionable parts of the capital. If the British paymasters didn't like anything Benes' people planned to do, they could stop it at once by turning off the cash. (In 1942 President Roosevelt suggested the same method to Churchill in order to bring 'Joan of Arc', as FDR called the French primadonna, Charles de Gaulle, to heel. Churchill refused.)

It is clear, therefore, that Benes could *not* have instigated an operation of such far-reaching magnitude, i.e. the assassination of Heydrich, without British permission and approval. So the question remains: who did approve the Heydrich mission? Victor (later Lord) Cavendish Bentinck, who was chairman of the Joint Intelligence Committee at that time, the body which had to approve all intelligence missions, maintained that his committee never even considered the matter.* Indeed, Cavendish Bentinck, who once appeared at General Patton's HQ in the field, clad as a typical Whitehall bureaucrat, complete with bowler, stated that he knew nothing of the mission until it was underway.

One must conclude, therefore, that the SIS ordered the operation. However, the SIS wouldn't carry it out; that would be left to the Czechs. After all the British Government, as stated by Lord Halifax back in 1939, 'did not use assassination as a substitute for diplomacy'. But things had changed drastically since then. In Berlin 'the poison dwarf' would soon ask the German nation to agree to 'total war', as if the Germans weren't already engaged in a life-and-death struggle in which no holds were barred. The time had come for a hard-pressed Britain to do so the same, even if total war went against all the principles of its thousand year old democracy.

But the British plotters made sure that the Germans would never be able to trace the coming murder back to the British government, even Churchill himself. Perhaps that was why the Joint Intelligence Committee never got wind of it until the assassination had been carried out. And to cover their tracks even further, the London plotters ordered Colonel Moravec, who would lead the operation, not to reveal to the Czech killers-to-be the name of their intended victim. The killers were to be given the name of several possible victims in their homeland but would be told the identity of the real target only when they reached Czechoslovakia.

That October Colonel Moravec received Gabcik and another Czech Army NCO Svoboda (soon to be replaced by Gabcik's friend Kubis) at his home in Rosendale Road, West Dulwich. Here he operated behind the cover of a radio shop run by SIS agent, Red Adams. From there they were driven to the Colonel's private office in Porchester Gate. Here Moravec briefed the two NCOs beginning with an emotional appeal:

*In a letter to the author.

The radio and newspapers have told you about the insane, murderous slaughter that is going on at home, in our own houses. The Germans are killing the finest men we have . . . our people have fought . . . now they are in a difficult position. It is our turn to help them from the outside. This October is the saddest October national holiday that our country has known since its independence – the holiday must be marked in a most outstanding fashion.

With the pep talk over, Colonel Moravec now came to the point:

It has been decided that it shall be done by a strike that will go down in history. In Prague there are two persons representative of the killings. They are K H Frank and the newcomer Heydrich . . . In the opinion of our leaders we must try to make one of them pay for all the rest, so as to prove that we return blow for blow. That is essentially the mission with which you have been entrusted.

Finally the British Government was going to fight the war in the shadows with the gloves off, though it was going to be these Czech pawns who would do the dirty work for them. The political assassinations had begun.

May 27 1942 dawned cold and a little hazy in Czechoslovakia. But by ten o'clock that morning, when Heydrich said good-bye to his wife and children at Penenske-Brezany, their house just outside Prague, it had become warm and sunny.

The night before, Heydrich had attended a concert devoted to the music of his father. Afterwards, there had been a reception and the new Reich Protector had drunk too much as he was wont to do. Now his head was heavy and he ordered his SS sergeant driver to keep the car's hood down. The fresh air would do him good. He had a busy day in front of him and on the morrow he would fly to Hitler's forward HQ to report to the Führer personally. There was talk of his being posted to France.

Now he sat next to his driver and closest to the pavement. Before the Germans had come the Czechs had driven on the left-hand side of the road. Within the first week of their occupation, the Germans had changed all that. The Czechs had been ordered to drive on the same side of the road as their German masters. The change was going to have a decisive effect on this day's events.

Ever since Gabcik and Kubis had been dropped in December 1941 under the cover of a snowstorm, they had been spying on Heydrich. Both of them were now living with Czech women, one of whom was pregnant. Wearing civilian clothes and equipped with Czech identity cards, they fitted well into the local scenery. Nothing marked them as potential assassins, trained NCOs, both of whom had won decorations for bravery during the fighting in France, back in 1940.

By now they had penetrated Heydrich's HQ at Prague's Hradcany Castle. There one of the servants had shown them the Protector's car and told them of his SS guard. 'White with fear', he explained, 'the whole thing stank of the graveyard.' They calmed him down and convinced the servant to pass out a note on Heydrich's daily movements every evening.

After a month, however, the two men concluded that Heydrich could not be killed at his estate or in the castle. Prague city centre was out too. In the end they started to concentrate on the road which Heydrich took daily to his office, trying to find the best spot to carry out their daring plan. But other problems began to impinge. The leaders of the Czech right-wing resistance loyal to the London Government in Exile had become aware of what Gabcik and Kubis were up to. In April 1942 they approached the two NCOs and told them of their fears of mass reprisals if Heydrich was murdered. As a member of the Resistance recalled after the war:

> The young men asserted that their mission was perfectly clear: they were to organise and carry out the killing. They were soldiers and could find no fault with the killing, or discuss its point or lack of point, or its timeliness or its untimeliness. At the most, they might think it over, but they could do nothing against an order that they had been given.

Frustrated and realising they could get no further with the two NCOs, the local Resistance signalled London:

> This assassination would not be of the least value to the Allies and for our nation it would have unforeseeable consequences. It would threaten not only hostages and political prisoners, but also thousands of other lives. The nation would be the subject of unheard-of reprisals. At the same time it would wipe out the remainders of our resistance ... Therefore we beg you to give the order for the assassination not to take place. Danger in delay. Give the order at once.

When the Resistance's message was received in London, there was a heated discussion about it in President Benes' office. In the presence of Colonel Moravec, they discussed what should be done; how they should reply to the frightened men in Prague.

There are two versions of what resulted. Perhaps Colonel Moravec's is the more accurate.

> I took the message to President Benes and then the Chief of the British Intelligence Service [General Menzies]. President Benes ordered me

not to answer [the Prague message]. The Chief of the SIS did not say anything, but I have learned since the war the British . . . insisted on the execution of the order.

Naturally he did. The men who ran Queen Anne's Gate, the then SIS HQ, were hard men. They wanted Heydrich dead. On 20 May Gabcik and Kubis received an order, via the SIS radio link, in a code that only they knew how to decipher. In vain the Czech Resistance tried to crack the code to find out what that order was. The attempt failed, but after the war the survivors of the Resistance said that they were sure that it was an order from London to kill Heydrich. According to one witness of the events in Prague at that time, Gabcik was heard to remark after he had deciphered the message from London, 'There is nothing else we can do because *the order has arrived.'*

Now time was running out fast for the two assassins. Their fellow Czech resisters were turning against them. They suspected that they might be betrayed to the Gestapo by their own people. It was clearly the only way that Gabcik and Kubis could be stopped now. The two assassins had also heard the rumours coming from circles in the capital that Heydrich, who was still running the German police apparatus in addition to his duties in Prague, might well be transferred elsewhere before the spring of 1942 was out.

In the end Kubis and Gabcik decided they'd kill Heydrich on the one day when they knew exactly what the German's movements would be – 27 May 1942. All the same they had still not found the ideal site to stage their ambush and carry out the assassination.

Finally they made a snap decision. They picked a spot in the Prague suburb of Holesovice. Here there was a crossroads with a sharp bend which led on to Traja Bridge. From the assassins' point of view the place had several advantages. At the bend Heydrich's SS driver would be forced to slow down. Here, too, the Heydrich car would be at its most vulnerable. It was quite a distance from Heydrich's home, where there were guards and also the Prague German garrison. Finally there were no Czech police posts (the Czech police mostly were loyal to their German masters) in the immediate area. So they would be able to escape quickly after the murder on their bicycles, heading through that well-populated area to one of the Czech Resistance's safe houses. And they knew that *after* the Heydrich assassination, the Czech Resistance wouldn't dare to abandon them.

It was a crude and hastily organised plan, worked out under intense pressure, but Gabcik and Kubis, plus two helpers, were confident it would work. In retrospect one could feel a great deal of sympathy for these young men planning to commit a murder despite everything being against them, including their own comrades in the Resistance. In essence they hadn't a real chance of escaping once the deed had been done. To what country could they flee? And in their homeland, small as it was and rife with informers and traitors, how long could they survive?* Yet they were determined to carry out their mission, come what may.

The four would-be assassins had been at their posts near the bend since nine o'clock that May morning. According to the schedule smuggled out of Prague to them, Heydrich's car should have made its appearance at eight. Now it was an hour late. Gabcik was posted on one side of the road with sten gun hidden under his coat. Kubis, for his part, lounged, or appeared to do so, on the other side, where the Dresden–Prague road ran down the slope to the sharp curve. In the distance, one of their helpers named Valcik was stationed. He was to signal Heydrich's approach down the hill with a mirror. Still he hadn't signalled yet.

Another tense fifteen minutes passed. Gabcik was just considering whether he should scrub the mission when he saw it. A bright flash of light. It was the signal. Heydrich was on his way. Almost immediately there was the roar of a speeding car. An abrupt crash of gears. A whine of protesting rubber. The driver was hitting the brakes to take the sharp bend. And there they were!

Klein, the SS driver, didn't notice the Czechs. Everything was as it always was. A tram was rumbling towards them. There were passengers waiting patiently for it to stop. Beyond, two Czech police in black went about their lawful duties. Nothing unusual, the SS NCO told himself.

Gabcik reacted first. He flung open his old white raincoat. Beneath it he gripped his sten gun. Based on a Czech design, the weapon was cheap and mass-produced, costing six shillings and eight pence. In the British Army, it was widely regarded as unreliable. Gabcik was confident his would work. He jerked back the trigger. At this range he couldn't miss. *Nothing*! There was no answering tremble of the little weapon which could be concealed by breaking it into three parts.

Abruptly Klein spotted the civilian armed with the machine pistol. Heydrich did the same a moment later. He yelled something. Then he made a fatal mistake. It was typical of his overweening arrogance. Instead of ordering Klein to drive on at top speed, he stood upright, yanked out his pistol and cried to Klein to brake. As always Heydrich believed rules were for other people, not for him. And one must admit, Reinhard Heydrich had always been brave.

It was the opportunity that Kubis had been waiting for. While Heydrich prepared to fire, believing that he was dealing with a single assassin, Kubis stepped out of the shadows and lobbed his grenade at the car. But instead of landing in the car as Kubis had planned, it hit the rear wheel.

It exploded immediately. Sharp metal shards pinged through the air.

*Slovakia, part of the old Czechoslovakia, had become a separate state and in the end Germany's ally, sending troops to Russia to fight alongside the Wehrmacht against the 'Bolsheviks'.

Kubis yelped as he was hit by one of them. Behind, the windows of the tram which had just come to a halt were shattered. There were screams as some of its passengers were hit. To the front the Mercedes lurched to a stop, its rear type ripped open and deflated.

But as the smoke cleared, the assassins saw to their horror that both of the car's occupants were on their feet and apparently uninjured. Not only that but both the Germans were getting out of the car, intent on fighting it out. Yelling at the top of his voice, Heydrich started uphill where Gabcik stood as if mesmerised. He was still holding his useless sten gun and now the Protector was preparing to fire. Klein was heading for Kubis. The latter was leaning weakly against some railings, half blinded by the blood pouring from the shrapnel wounds in his head.

Then Kubis realised the danger he was in. He staggered towards his old bike. Shouting at the top of his voice, he pushed his way through the crowd of shocked tram passengers. To lend urgency to his flight, he pulled out his old Colt pistol and fired a couple of shots into the air. The passengers scattered. Klein raised his automatic. He fired. At that range the NCO shouldn't have missed, but he did.

Now Klein pressed the magazine-release button by mistake. The pistol jammed. Minutes later Kubis was sailing down the hill on his bike towards the sanctuary of a safe house.

Now Klein turned his attention to Gabcik, as Heydrich yelled a little weakly: 'Get the bastard!' Heydrich staggered against the bonnet of the wrecked car, as Klein set off. He knew he was losing consciousness, but none of the Czechs stepped forward to help him.

Klein was closing on Gabcik. The latter ran into a butcher's shop. Its owner, Brauer, was a Nazi sympathiser. He fled his shop, crying that there was an armed man inside. Klein's pistol still would not work. Still he came on. Gabcik fired twice at the SS man. Klein went down wounded in both legs. The Czech assassin saw a moving tram. The conductor, a loyal Czech, saw the fugitive. He opened a side door. Gabcik sprang inside. He thrust the pistol inside his pocket. The tram was crowded, but no one seemed to notice him. Twenty minutes later he was in a safe house, rinsing his hair with camomile lotion to remove the substance with which he had dyed it, believing that he had failed. Heydrich was still alive . . .

Heydrich fought for his life for eight days. Hitler personally sent doctors to Prague to try to save him. To no avail. Later it was stated that the grenade which had wounded him had been impregnated with anthrax spores for which there was no cure.

At 4.30 a.m. on 4 June 1942, Heydrich died. As Benes and the Czech Resistance had anticipated, the Germans took a terrible revenge, in particular they wiped out the village of Lidice, killing a total of 172 men and boys. The female population of the village was sent to Ravensbruck Concentration Camp where most of them perished. Some ninety children from the village, who were thought worthy of becoming German citizens, were sent to be adopted in the Reich. Only a few ever returned. Perhaps today there are elderly people in Germany who think themselves German, but who are in reality the only survivors of that doomed village.*

'The Massacre of Lidice' became the first recorded German atrocity of WWII, recorded because the German authorities wanted it to serve as a warning to others. According to German sources, some 10,000 Czechs were arrested, of whom 1,300 were shot or murdered, including Gabcik and Kubis who died in a Prague shoot-out with the SS, whereupon their heads were severed and exhibited. For a while production figures sank in Bohemia and Moravia as a result of the German wave of terror, but only for a while. Although Jan Masaryk, the son of the founder of Czecho-slovakia, maintained that after the Heydrich murder, 'Czechoslovakia was put on the map again and we had an easy time', the country con-tinued to produce armoured vehicles and guns for the Wehrmacht right up to April–May 1945. Today those same car works belong to German automobile manufacturers and are again working for German industry (much to the chagrin of native German workers, who fear for their jobs, it must be said).

Back in London, the Foreign Office was careful to avoid any direct endorsement of the Heydrich murder. The word was out that it was to be regarded as an internal Czech matter. As Frank Roberts of the Central Department recorded on 11 June 1942: 'However much we may welcome Heydrich's fate, it is not, I imagine, the policy of HM Government to go out of their way to glorify political assassinations'.**

Undoubtedly it was not the policy of HM Government to glorify political assassination. What could be achieved by it? After all Britain was a democracy, purporting to uphold the sanctity of human life. When the Germans made public the dreadful reprisals that they had wreaked on the Czechs after the Heydrich murder, their declarations served a purpose. They frightened the Czechs into accepting their lot tamely and at the same time ensured the co-operation of the Czech labour force working in the vital armaments industry in that country.

Whoever ordered the assassination of Reinhard Heydrich remains a mystery to this day. But it is clear that an act of such magnitude could not

*For a while the village of Lidice gained worldwide prominence. Hollywood made a movie about the massacre, a Welsh village named itself after the Czech village, and for several years after the war good people in England and Wales helped to pay for the village's restoration. Today Lidice is forgotten.
**Some researchers have identified the Briton who devised the plan to kill Heydrich as 52-year-old, kilt-wearing John Skinner Wilson, who after retiring from the Indian Police spent most of his life working for the Boy Scout movement. Indeed he was the director of Boy Scouts International before he joined the SOE. From 1 Jan. 1942 to 1945 he was head of the SOE's Danish section.

have been carried out without the approval and permission of those at the very top in Britain. The Germans must have thought so. For now as 1942 gave way to 1943 and Britain had seemingly broken the unspoken agreement not to kill German political leaders, it was not surprising that the Germans set about getting rid of the Third Reich's most implaceable enemy: the one Hitler thought had kept Britain at war with the Third Reich back in 1940 when it had been clear to any sensible person, save that 'drunken sot in London' (as Hitler routinely called him contemptuously), that Britain had lost it. Now it was the turn of Winston Spencer Churchill!

When in 1939 Winston Churchill returned from the political wilderness to become First Lord of the Admiralty, he brought with him his long-term bodyguard Walter Thompson of Scotland Yard's Special Branch. Inspector Thompson, tall with an angular tough face, had been in the bodyguard business since WWI and had accompanied Churchill on his American lecture tour of 1931–2. Four years later he retired from the police to become a greengrocer until Churchill joined the government and asked the Inspector to become his bodyguard once more.

The job was no sinecure. Churchill, even later as Prime Minister, had no special bodyguard unit, unlike Hitler with his Führerbegleitkommando and a whole household of armed servants (even his butler Heinz Linge was a colonel in the SS and always carried a pistol with him). Churchill's basic security was left to Thompson and his relief detective.

But whereas Hitler was a fatalist, as we have seen, and thought that a determined assassin would be able to get through his security screen if he tried hard enough, Churchill believed he and Thompson could see off any would-be murderer without any help. Churchill, on the whole, appeared to ignore the many death threats made against him during the war. But by the time he had become Prime Minister in May 1940, he had, on Thompson's advice, taken to carrying a pistol and practising with it on the range under Thompson's instruction.

Once around that period, when Mrs Churchill asked her husband if the Nazis would invade Britain, Churchill grinned and, according to Thompson, answered. 'No. But they'll make a mighty good try. At least I would if I were Hitler.' Thereupon, Churchill opened his coat briefly and displayed his revolver, saying, 'If they do try, I'll get a few before they take me.'

Although Hitler appeared to be fatalistic about his life, he did take his personal precautions, especially when he was at his new Chancellery in Berlin. As ex-Obersturmbannführer Gerd Bremer related:*

All the sentries of the Leibstandarte close to Hitler's quarters were supposed to stand guard with a loaded pistol in their hands. Once

*To the author.

Hitler crept out of his bedroom at night and found a soldier asleep. He took the man's pistol and told me as officer in charge to return the pistol to the man the following morning. The young soldier was so ashamed that he shot himself.

Churchill, on the other hand, didn't appear to regard this self-defence business as too important. He decided to start carrying a heavy Colt .45 for his protection. It was a much heavier weapon than that carried by Thompson, and Churchill would prance around as if he were an excited, overgrown schoolboy playing cowboys and Indians, shooting another imaginary 'pesky Redskin'. Then the Colt became too heavy for him and he'd forget it deliberately so that Thompson would be forced to lend the PM one of his small calibre revolvers.

Even when Churchill went on one of his many foreign trips to dangerous places, including several battlefields, he would wander around, even late at night, accompanied only by Thompson and a couple of soldiers, with seemingly not a care in the world. Ex-Sergeant Danny Mander, now a US citizen, remembers guarding the PM in Teheran in '43 when Churchill attended a conference of the 'Big Three'. Allied Intelligence knew, as we shall see, that the Germans were dropping parachute agents to kill the Allied leaders. According to the sergeant in the Military Politary Police, as Mander was then, Churchill decided to go for a walk. As Mander recalled:

> I accompanied him like a faithful dog, lagging a few paces behind. As he walked, he commented about flowers and trees along the paths. I occasionally replied to prevent it sounding as though he was talking to himself.

It was on that November day that Churchill sauntered through the British Legation garden, accompanied only by an inexperienced bodyguard and seemingly totally at ease and unaware of any danger to his person, that Colonel Joseph Spencer in charge of British security in the Persian capital caught the first of the would-be German assassins. They came floating out of the sky, flown to Persia in long-range German Condor planes, right into the arms of Spencer's special agents.

It was clear by 1943 that the unspoken truce between Germany and Britain (that neither side should attempt to assassinate the other country's political leaders) had come to an end. Perhaps the cold-blooded and calculated murder of Heydrich which had angered Hitler greatly had made the Führer change his mind on that subject. At all events, the middle year of the war marked a turning point in the nasty business of killing one's political opponents on the other side. For already in June '43, five months before that episode in Teheran, it must have been clear to Churchill that the German enemy was plotting against his life.

That June Churchill was doing one of his customary tours of the front, in particular, North Africa. As usual with the PM it was part propaganda, an exercise in morale by letting the troops see him and his need to find out what was really going on by talking to the men on the spot.

At the same time as Churchill was doing his bit in North Africa, another well-known Briton was doing the same on the other side of the Mediterranean, name in Portugal. If Churchill epitomised the 'Bulldog' spirit, this other Englishman seemed the quintessential British gentleman. He was Leslie Howard, the gifted and extremely English actor, who had played the character of Ashley Wilkes in the 1939 classic *Gone With the Wind*.

Since that record-breaking Hollywood movie, Howard, now aged 50, had done his part in publicising his country's cause in such films as *Pimpernel Smith* (1941), in which Smith-Howard delays the invasion of Poland and delivers a homily to the audience on the meaning of the war. He makes it clear that there will be an ultimate victory of the weak (but morally strong) over the strong (but morally weak). For the time, although the story was very unlikely, it sent a stirring, seductive message to the audience. Thereafter had followed such movies the *First of the Few* (1942), and the *Gentle Sex* (1943).

Now this May–June, Howard had been lecturing for four weeks in Spain and Portugal, while his film, *First of the Few*, depicting the life of the inventor of the war-winning Spitfire aircraft, H J Mitchell, was showing in Portuguese cinemas.

The tour was now over and Howard and his manager Alfred Chenhalls, who looked and dressed like Churchill and smoked large cigars as the PM did, waited for a plane to take them from Lisbon to England. With them were waiting a strange bunch of characters, who might well have come out of one of the Hollywood spy movies of the time. There was a supposed mining engineer, who specialised in finding tungsten, a vital metal for the British war industry; a Jewish intelligence operative who smuggled Jews out of Germany to be questioned in the UK by British Intelligence; a British consular corps official on a 'routine inspection tour', among others.

All of them were nervous as they waited for the unarmed airliner which would transport them home. Howard was no exception. He had been talked into the Iberian lecture tour by his manager and no less a person than Foreign Secretary Anthony Eden. Howard thought the trip 'arduous, dangerous and of minuscule importance' to the British war effort. Still he had done as ordered, although he knew that he was particularly hated by the Nazis because of his BBC radio broadcasts beamed to Germany defending democracy and human rights and attacking the Nazi creed.

But all of them, this mixed bunch of foreigners and Britishers with dubious backgrounds, had good reason to fear what might lie ahead. Then they were about to undertake a flight in an unarmed civilian aircraft along the western coast of German-occupied Europe. In particular, their plane would cross the Bay of Biscay, guarded by the Junkers 88s of the newly formed German Kampfgeschwader 40. Its fighter-bombers flew far out into the Atlantic to protect the German U-boats sailing to and from their French bases. What if these junkers took their civilian plane for one of the RAF aircraft which routinely bombed the area?

Besides the Germans knew everything about these dangerous unarmed flights from Lisbon to the UK. As Harry Pusey, BOAC's Operations Officer in the Portuguese capital at that time, recalled: '[Lisbon] was like Casablanca, but multiplied twenty-fold . . . The place was crawling with spies, British, German, Soviet and American.'

Since the majority of Pusey's passengers were VIPs, the Germans were always trying to find out who was on the passenger lists. Their spies invariably hovered about the British Terminal (next to the German one incidentally) trying to get a glimpse of the passengers so that they could report to the German Legation's Abwehr agent who they were.

Pusey always tried to trail these men and the German Lufthansa pilots, many of whom he knew from pre-war days. Now as 1 June 1943 approached and the passengers were being readied for the flight to Whitchurch near Bristol, Pusey was worried that some of them were dropping out without any real explanation. Indeed one was a Catholic priest who benefited from a mysterious anonymous phone call summoning him back to the Portuguese capital. Later it was supposed that ULTRA already knew of the German plans for the plane that would take Howard home, but that the pilot and passengers couldn't be warned in case the great decoding operation was compromised. Seemingly the priest might have profited from some leak in the ULTRA secret distribution list in Lisbon.

Howard's plane, named the 'Ibis', was one of four KLM DC3s which had been the only survivors of the German bombing of Schipol Airport outside Amsterdam back in May 1940. Now for two and a half years the planes and their Dutch crews had worked this shuttle service between Portugal and Whitchurch on behalf of the British government. In contrast the British authorities provided the York which was about to fly Churchill back home from North Africa with an escort of Spitfires for at least part of the way. Captain Tepes, the Dutch pilot of the 'Ibis', carrying Howard and the Churchill lookalike, Howard's manager Chenhalls, were not so lucky.

Perhaps all those ill-fated men, women and children (there were two aboard the doomed aircraft) should have known and taken heed of the ancient Egyptian belief that the 'souls of the dead just pass from earth to heaven on the wings of the ibis' (*The Book of the Dead*). What was about to happen now would eerily confirm the apparent wisdom of that ancient Egyptian belief.

Just before the 'Ibis' departed, Harry Pusey heard that the 'word on the street' was that a German agent had spotted Howard at the airport and got the message to the German authorities that he was the real Mitchell (i.e. the inventor of the Spitfire whose biopic was currently being shown in Lisbon with Leslie Howard in the starring role). As a result Howard was picked as a target for German assassination, though as Pusey remarked many years later, 'but you would have thought that someone in German Intelligence would have known that Mitchell had died in 1937, wouldn't you?' Subsequent events, however, would show it wasn't the dead Mitchell the Germans were after but Chenhalls, Howard's manager, who unfortunately for him and his boss, looked so like the British Prime Minister.

At 9.40 a.m. on Tuesday 1 June 1943 the 'Ibis' took off. On board the BOAC Dakota there were seventeen people, thirteen passengers – a bad omen in itself – and four crew members. Three hours later at 12.54 p.m., flying over the water at 1,000 feet and with the Spanish peninsula some two hundred miles behind it, the Dutch captain radioed a chilling message in code. 'From G-AGBB [the plane's call sign], I am followed by an unidentified aircraft . . .' Moments later came the signal, 'I am attacked by enemy aircraft.' After that there were no more calls from the plane.

After the war captured Luftwaffe documents revealed what had happened. That afternoon a squadron of six Junkers was patrolling the area under the command of a Leutnant Herbert Hinze. About midday, one of the German pilots signalled his commander, 'Indians at eleven o'clock'. Hinze spotted the 'Indian'. It was a twin-engined aircraft and Hinze thought it strange that it was both unarmed and unescorted. But before the commander could do anything about it, one of his pilots, assuming the plane belonged to the RAF and diving steeply, let loose with his machine guns. His bullets struck the port engine and set it afire immediately.

As the Dakota went into a long curving dive of death, Hinze spotted three parachutes blossom out as three of the unknown people aboard 'hit the silk'. He ordered an immediate ceasefire. Too late. The plane plunged into the sea. Returning to their French base, the unhappy pilots discovered they had shot down an unarmed civilian airliner. Later Hinze maintained that he and his men were angry at the news. They were new to this posting and no one had briefed them that there was a regular civilian air connection between Lisbon and Britain. Angry, too, at the information that the British authorities had allowed such a slow unarmed aeroplane to fly through this area of extremely dangerous air space.

But by then it was too late. For several days the RAF searched the area for wreckage or any sign of survivors. As Flight-Lieutenant Kneald recorded:'* We weren't told anything about Mr Howard or any of the

---

*To the author.

other passengers for that matter, only that it was important to find some trace of the Dakota having been shot down.' But they never did. After three days the RAF searchers gave up. As far as Flight-Lieutenant Kneald was concerned, the whole 'business remained shrouded in official secrecy' until after the war when he learned the truth.

> Then I found out that Mr Churchill was supposed by the Germans to have been on the downed plane and I presume our people wanted proof of the Huns' *Schrecklichkeit*, though of course the real victims were Leslie Howard, the actor and those poor little girls.

Whatever 'our people' wanted to prove, it was clear that the Germans had not been as innocent as Leutnant Hinze maintained after the war. It is obvious that the Germans thought Churchill had somehow come to Lisbon from North Africa and had been on the Dakota when it had flown from the Portuguese capital. This had been a golden opportunity, they must have reasoned, to get rid of the leader who, Hitler believed, had kept Britain in the war when she had been virtually defeated back in 1940. Now in 1943 Churchill was encouraging the new ally, the United States, to make the defeat of Germany its main concern. Moreover this new ally was dependent on Churchill's island as a kind of aircraft carrier for launching its own forces against Germany's Festung Europa. Then without Britain just off the coast of Europe, the USA, some 5,000 kilometres away, would not have possessed a viable launching pad. Get rid of Churchill, the creator of the so-called 'special relationship' between the UK and USA, and President Roosevelt might instead have turned his attention to the threat in the Pacific posed by Japan.

Those in the Allied camp were in no doubt that Churchill had been the Germans' target. Imprisoned Raymond Falla, the Chief Guernsey Agricultural Officer, then a prisoner of the German occupiers, remembers his German guards celebrating the 'death' of PM Churchill that June.

Inspector Thompson wrote later of the incident: 'We were delayed a day in our official plans to get back to England and there has been speculation all over the world that this delay saved Winston Churchill's life.' As 'Tommy' Thompson, Churchill's bodyguard, saw it:

> A civil aircraft flying to England from Lisbon – a plane similar to ours – was shot down over our route and about the same time the day before. One of the passengers was the famous actor, Leslie Howard, whom Winston had seen perform many times and some of whose films he owned and frequently showed in his private projection theatre at Chartwell. It occurred to us all at the time: Was that plane mistaken for ours? We were actually supposed to be at that spot at that time and even at that altitude.

But if Winston Churchill that summer was primarily concerned with the first invasion of Hitler's Festung Europa, namely the Allied attack on Sicily scheduled during his visit to North Africa for July 1943, he did recall in one of his books, *The Hinge of Fate* (1950), that incident of long before. In the book Churchill regarded the mistaken identity thesis (i.e. Howard's companion Alfred Chenhalls being mistaken for himself) as proven fact. He referred to Leslie Howard's death at the hands of the Germans as one of 'the inscrutable workings of fate'.

One thing is certain. Thereafter the courageous old man always kept a Thompson sub-machine gun behind the door of his residence at Chartwell.

CHAPTER III
Enter Otto Skorzeny

'You have carried out a mission which will go down in history'.

Adolf Hitler

There was little in Otto Skorzeny's early life to give a clue as to why he should become the 'most dangerous man in Europe', as Supreme Commander General Eisenhower would call him during the war. He was born on 12 June 1908 into a typical middle-class Viennese family which had suffered badly after Austria's defeat in WWI when the Austrian currency was not worth the paper it was printed on. For a time the Skorzeny children only survived thanks to the efforts of the International Red Cross, which fed them as it did many other starving European kids.

Otto's boyhood ran through the worst years of the Depression in Austria and Central Europe. He remembered his father, whose business as an engineer suffered through a lack of capital and the poor value of the Austrian Schilling, telling him about the need for self-discipline. As young Otto tasted butter for the first time at the age of 15, he was told by his parent that there was 'no harm doing without things. It might even be a good thing not to get used to a soft life'.* It was advice and an exercise in self-discipline that would come in useful to the teenager who was beginning to grow into a giant – in later life he was six foot four and broadly built with it.

Perhaps, however, it was his first encounter with the traditional student duelling societies at the University of Vienna – he had enrolled there at the age of 18 to study engineering – which marked the first really decisive influence on his life. At that time the traditional German and Austrian universities had cultivated the 'art' of duelling with a heavy sabre for over a century.

The University of Vienna was no exception. There the *schlagende Verbindungen* (duelling societies) flourished and Otto Skorzeny was soon an enthusiastic member of one such which met in one of the garden cafes of suburban Vienna, complete with ritualistic duelling and gigantic drinking bouts.

*To the author.

As Skorzeny was to comment in the years to come:

> I could feel my heart beating rapidly [during such fencing bouts]. I
> could only see the face of my opponent very vaguely through the
> steel grill of my mask. Blade against blade! ... With only the
> occasional pause while the blade of my sabre was disinfected. Then
> suddenly after the seventh round, I felt a short, sharp blow on my
> head. Surprisingly enough it didn't hurt too much. My only fear was
> that I had flinched.

Skorzeny had not.

Thereafter he fought thirteen more duels with other students which
resulted in his achieving the desired *Schmisse*, or scars, which marked him
as a university man who had absolved the bloody ritual of an academic
duelling society. Those scars would also gain him the nickname 'Scarface'
(after the pre-war Hollywood gangster movie of the same name starring
Viennese actor Paul Muni) in the Allied camp when he had become
notorious.

But for Otto Skorzeny duelling was more than just obtaining the much
sought after *Schmisse*. As he was to comment later:

> I was often grateful later for the self-discipline we learned in our
> student club. I never felt so bad under fire as I did at 18 when I had to
> fight my first duel under the sharp eyes of my fellow students . . . And
> just as in duelling you must fix your mind on striking at the enemy's
> head so, too, in war. You cannot waste time on feinting and
> sidestepping. You must decide on your target and go in.

It was advice he would follow strictly in the two and a half years as head
of the equivalent of Britain's SAS, only the 'heads' that Skorzeny went
after were those of heads of state!

When war came, Austria was already the 'Ostmark', part of the Third
Reich and its citizens were eligible for conscription. Not that Skorzeny, a
31-year-old engineer and a member of the Nazi Party, waited to be
conscripted. He volunteered immediately for the Luftwaffe, hoping to be
commissioned as a pilot.

He was fated to be disappointed. After five months' training he was told
he was too old and fit only for ground duties. That did it. Skorzeny
volunteered immediately for the elite of the elite, SS Leibstandarte Adolf
Hitler, the premier SS division bearing the name 'Hitler's Bodyguard'.

Only twelve of the men who volunteered at that time were accepted and
Skorzeny was one of them. He was posted as an ordinary recruit to the
division's 'Moonlight Company', named after its CO's unpleasant habit of
carrying out most of the company's training at night. Despite his age,

Skorzeny coped well and was soon promoted to *Fahnrich*, a kind of officer-cadet, in which rank he was transferred to SS Division 'Das Reich' to prove himself in combat before he was commissioned.

Thereafter the scarfaced giant saw action in the Balkans, was promoted and became an engineer officer in charge of ensuring the Division's tanks were always battle-worthy. In December 1941 the Division was engaged in the great winter battle in Russia when Skorzeny was hit in the head by a mortar fragment and knocked out.

When he came to, a soldier handed him a cigarette and a glass of schnapps. He refused any medical treatment although he was wounded and carried on until persistent headaches and a bad case of what the SS called 'thin shits', i.e. a stomach colic, forced his evacuation to Germany for specialised treatment. That was the end of his career with a regular military formation with its tight discipline, rules and regulations. Now, though the sick lieutenant didn't know it at the time, Skorzeny was heading for a spectacularly unorthodox military career which, even in his wildest dreams, he could never have imagined would be his.

In early 1942 Skorzeny was summoned from the Leibstandarte's depot in Berlin to meet an officer, who explained he had come back to Germany to set up a commando troop on the British lines for irregular warfare. Did Skorzeny want to join this new formation? The Austrian giant didn't take long to make up his mind, and there was nothing subtle in his reasoning. 'For anyone with blood in his veins,' he explained later, 'there is, at certain turning points, only one way to go. A man who can still see the choice of two roads then may be a clever fellow – I could not say much more for him.'

Several months later, on 18 April 1943, Otto Skorzeny, newly promoted to the rank of Hauptsturmführer der Reserve, became the head of Germany's first special troops, das Friedenthaler Jagdkommando, the Friedenthal Hunting Group* outside Berlin.

On 25 July he was taking his ease with an old Viennese acquaintance at the capital's posh Hotel Eden. After a few *Kognaks* he decided it was time to report in to his HQ at Friedenthal. When he did, his female secretary was on the verge of panic. For two long hours the whole place had been searching for him. When a perplexed Skorzeny enquired why, his secretary yelled shrilly: 'Chief, they want you at the Führer's head-quarters.'

Skorzeny understood his secretary's panic. So far no one from Jagdkommando Friedenthal had ever been summoned to the Führer's HQ. The balloon must have really gone up. Hastily he asked: 'Have you any indication what this is about?'

His secretary answered in the negative. Totally unprepared for what

---

*Named after the place where they were based.

was to come, Skorzeny set off for the 'Wolf's Lair'.* He had expected it to be a rough-and-ready place. Instead it turned out to be a small village of camouflaged huts and concrete bunkers set in the middle of a forest, guarded by an SS battalion and several score anti-aircraft guns. But he had no time to wonder about the place. Almost immediately he was ushered into an ante-room, where six other officers waited nervously. Skorzeny guessed they were there for the same reason he was.

In the end they were ushered into the map room, decorated solely by a sand table. Hitler entered a few moments later. The officers snapped to attention. In silence the Führer mustered them one by one before asking somewhat surprisingly, 'which of you knows Italy?'

Skorzeny, the most junior officer present, was the only one to reply: 'Mein Führer,' he said, 'I have been through Italy twice as far as Naples on my motorcycle.'

Hitler nodded and then asked, 'What do you think of the Italians?'

The other men gave various answers: 'Axis partners . . . Members of the Anti-Comintern Pact . . . Germany's ally.'

But when it came to Skorzeny's turn to answer, he said to his fellow Austrian Hitler, 'I am an Austrian, mein Führer'.

He felt that should suffice. Hitler, an Austrian citizen until he became a German in 1928, should know what he felt about a nation which, in his opinion, had seized one of the most beautiful parts of their native land, the South Tyrol, following WWI.

Hitler stared up at the giant Viennese for what seemed to Skorzeny a very long time before saying, 'The other gentlemen can go. I want to speak to you, however, Hauptsturmführer Skorzeny. 'As the others filed out, as mystified as ever, Skorzeny felt flattered that the Führer could at least pronounce his difficult name correctly.

As soon as the others had departed, Hitler got down to business. He said: 'I have a very important commission for you. Mussolini, my friend and our loyal comrade-in-arms, was betrayed yesterday by his king and was arrested by his own countrymen.' Swiftly Hitler explained that secret negotiations between the Western Allies, now ready to land in mainland Italy, and the Italian Badoglio faction, had resulted in a decision to surrender Italy to the former. One of the details worked out by the new 'Badoglio Government' with the Western powers had been to arrest the Duce, Mussolini. Hitler said: 'To me the Duce is the incarnation of the ancient grandeur of Rome. Italy under the new government will desert us. I will keep faith with my old ally and dear friend. He must be rescued promptly or he will be handed over the Allies.'

Hardly allowing time for his words to sink in, Hitler added: 'I herewith

*In the early days of his political career, Hitler had used the name 'Doctor Wolf'. Hence the name given to several of his HQs.

46

order you to carry out this task, which is vital for the war. You must do everything in your power to carry it out. And if you do, then you will be successful.'

Skorzeny was so bemused that all he could think of to say was the customary soldier's response to an order he didn't quite understand: 'Jawohl, mein Führer.'

Hitler accepted the reply as agreement. He snapped:

> Now the main points. You must keep the mission secret, Skorzeny. Only five other people apart from yourself will know of it. You will turn to the Luftwaffe for the operation. I have already informed General Student.* Discuss the matter with him. He'll give you the details. It's up to *you* to find out where the Duce is. And once again, absolute secrecy. I hope to hear from you soon and would like to wish you all the best.

With that Hitler dismissed him. But hardly had Skorzeny been dismissed than a Luftwaffe adjutant said, 'General Student would like to see you now.'

The great Mussolini rescue operation, which would make Skorzeny famous (some would say infamous) throughout the world, was under way.

The start of the operation had been set for dawn. But the gliders Student's paras would be using were delayed on their flight to Italy from France. At first Skorzeny, down below at the base of the Italian Gran Sasso mountain where the Italians were holding the Duce prisoner, was angry at the hitch. Now he calmed down, reasoning that the gliders would arrive at an ideal time – noon. Then the Italian guards, stuffed with a heavy lunch and wine, wouldn't expect anyone in his right mind to attack at that time of the day.

The hours passed leadenly. It was a beautiful September day in the mountains, bright and windless, ideal for the combined land and airborne operation. Now after weeks of searching for the missing Italian dictator, Skorzeny felt that this time he would succeed. To keep his men happy, the Viennese giant passed through the ranks of his heavily armed men handing out fruit like some Italian street peddlar.

Then it was 12.30. The gliders had landed. Now they were drawn up, ready for the paras to board them. In thirty minutes they would

---

*Student was the head of the German Paratroop Corps, which came under the orders of the Luftwaffe at this time. In due course he became Skorzeny's enemy, maintaining that the Austrian used his paras for his own personal glory. In his old age Student told the author he thought Skorzeny a 'parvenu', who 'risked other people's lives [i.e. his paras'] in order to make a name for himself.'

commence the operation. Skorzeny prayed that the 'Macaronis' up there in the mountain hotel where they held their prisoner wouldn't put up more than a token resistance; after all the place was built like a fortress with excellent fields of fire.

Suddenly, startlingly, the air raid sirens started to wail their dread warning. Skorzeny cursed. Almost immediately Allied medium bombers came winging low over the airfield where the gliders were drawn up. Bombs fell everywhere. In a flash the attackers had completed their bombing run and were winging their way high into the steel-blue sky over the mountain. But when the smoke had cleared, an anxious Skorzeny saw to his relief that none of the precious gliders had been hit. Now there was no time to be lost. The enemy bombers would soon be reporting the presence of German gliders on the little field.

He pushed the flustered Italian general, whom they had forced to come with them, in between Skorzeny's legs in the front seat of one of the frail gliders. He glanced at his watch. One o'clock. The guards would have eaten. It was time to go. He gave the signal. The engines of the tows started to roar. They had lift-off heading for the bank of cloud which blotted out all sight at 9,000 feet.

Up and up they went. As Skorzeny recalled, 'the interior of the glider was unpleasantly hot and stuffy . . . I suddenly noticed that the corporal behind me was being sick and the general in front had turned as green as his uniform.'

But Skorzeny had other things to worry about. The thick celluloid windows of the DFS glider were difficult to see through and the pilot was flying blind, relying on Skorzeny's knowledge of the route to guide him to Gran Sasso. It was about that time that the pilot of the Henschel towing Skorzeny's plane reported he had lost the lead planes, asking, 'Who is to take over now?'

'We'll take over,' Skorzeny responded immediately. Taking out his dagger, he hacked at the canvas deck and wall. Cool mountain air rushed in. The men's air sickness vanished at once. Minutes later, with Skorzeny peering out of his peephole to guide the remaining gliders, they spotted the hotel where the Duce was held prisoner. 'Helmets on,' he ordered urgently. 'Slip the tow ropes.'

There was a sudden silence. The tow rope had been cut. They were on their own. Now Skorzeny strained his eyes to find the DZ. He spotted it and gasped with shock. The landing patch was very steep and littered with large boulders. But there was no turning back now. 'Crash landing,' he ordered. 'Get as near to the hotel as possible.' The plane started downwards at a very steep angle. The strain on the flimsy glider was tremendous. Indeed Skorzeny wondered how the wood and canvas aircraft didn't disintegrate. It didn't. Moments later, Leutnant Meyer, the pilot, released the parachute break. The frail plane hit the alpine meadow.

There was a splintering of wood, the ripping of canvas. Then with one last mighty heave the glider slewed to a stop.

The paras tumbled out of the wrecked glider. The hotel was some fifteen metres away. An Italian soldier stood on the steps staring at them open-mouthed, as if he couldn't believe the evidence of his own eyes. But so far neither he nor anyone else had fired a shot at the assault party.

Skorzeny didn't give the Italians a chance to do so. He charged forward. Behind him came Student's paras. A face peered down at him as he rushed to the hotel's steps. It was that of Il Duce. He had found Mussolini at last. Ignoring the Italian soldiers who were everywhere now, Skorzeny skidded to a stop on the marble floor inside the hotel. In his poor Italian, he bellowed, 'I want the commander . . . He must come here at once.' Some bewildered shouting and then a bareheaded colonel sporting a spectacular moustache appeared. Skorzeny spelled out his demand:

> I ask your immediate surrender. Mussolini is in our hands. We hold the building. If you want to avert senseless bloodshed, you have sixty seconds to go and reflect.

Skorzeny need not have worried, although he was outnumbered. The colonel with the moustache disappeared and returned carrying a large glass of red wine in both hands. With a slight bow, he offered it to a Skorzeny, saying, 'To the victor.'

Skorzeny had achieved the virtually impossible. With a handful of men, he had discovered the new Italy's most important political prisoner and freed him from captivity. Now part of Italy at least would remain in the war and allow the Germans to fight the length of the Italian boot for nearly two more years, inflicting severe casualties on the Western Allies and the varied national formations from Basutos to Brazilians who would fight under Anglo-American command.

From the moment that Mussolini stared up at the scarfaced SS man, who seemingly had appeared out of nowhere and cried, 'I knew my friend Adolf Hitler would not leave me in the lurch', before embracing Skorzeny, the latter must have known that his whole life had changed. Now leaving an angry Student behind with his paras, he insisted that the General's personal pilot, Captain Gerlach, should fly him and Mussolini out.

Gerlach protested it was too dangerous. Skorzeny would have none of it. They flew out. A few hours later Skorzeny and Mussolini were in Vienna's Imperial Hotel – and the congratulations started to flow in.

Just after the head of the SS, Heinrich Himmler, had called to congratulate him, a tall, full colonel of the SS entered his room, with the medal of the Knight's Cross dangling from his throat. Almost wordlessly he took off the coverted decoration and placed it around Skorzeny's bull-like neck. 'On the Führer's order,' the colonel barked. Skorzeny in SS parlance had his 'cured throat ache' for his daring rescue of Il Duce. For the first time in the history of Germany's highest decoration, a soldier had been awarded it and given it on the same day that he had won it to another man.

Hardly had Skorzeny recovered from his surprise at the colonel handing over his own medal, than the phone rang again. It was the Führer himself. 'Today,' he said happily from his headquarters in East Prussia, 'you have carried out a mission which will go down in history. You have given me back my old friend Mussolini. I have given you the Knight's Cross and promoted you.' Thereafter 'Fat Hermann', roly-poly Hermann Goering, head of the Luftwaffe, took over the phone. He added his own congratulations. Field Marshal Keitel, Hitler's Chief-of-Staff followed. It seemed the whole of the Nazi *Prominenz* around the Führer were clamouring to congratulate the new hero. For an obscure officer of the Waffen SS, which Skorzeny had been only twenty-four hours before, it must all have been very heady stuff.

And the festivities, honours, celebrations, award ceremonies, even parades, did not cease there. Goering came to Vienna personally in his special train 'Amerika' to award Skorzeny the Air Force Medal in Gold (much to the chagrin of General Student, whose paras had done the hard work). Mussolini gave him something called the 'Order of the Hundred Musketeers'. Later in Berlin Skorzeny himself held a medal award ceremony in the capital's Sports Palace where he handed out medals to the paras who had assisted him on the Gran Sasso. The *Prominenz* fell over themselves to invite Skorzeny into their homes – Ribbentrop, Hitler's foreign minister, Bormann, his sinister secretary, Goebbels, Hitler himself – they all requested his company at informal gatherings. Otto Skorzeny was well on his way to becoming a social lion.

And indeed, Skorzeny, whose daring rescue of Mussolini had even been mentioned in the British House of Commons, had unwittingly shown the world a new way of conducting irregular warfare. Although his own Jagdkommando had been modelled on David Stirling's SAS, Skorzeny had focussed, and would concentrate on different and much more politically significant objects than the SAS. In essence, Colonel Stirling's men had attacked tactical objectives – airfields, storage depots, beaches and the like. Skorzeny had shown in one stroke that by rescuing Mussolini he had altered the whole nature of covert operations; he had changed the entire course of the war in Italy politically and militarily.*

Everywhere outside Germany, shrewd observers of the military scene realised that Skorzeny had just shown the world a new way of conducting

---

*Mussolini went on to found a new mini-state in Northern Italy and form a new Italian fascist army, numbering several divisions which lasted until the end of the war.

war. The Viennese ex-engineer, who was obviously not constrained by the conventional thinking of the regular soldier, had added a new dimension to modern warfare. The British and their Czech allies had made a clumsy and ill-fated sally into the same field with their murder of Reinhard Heydrich. But it hadn't really worked and it had certainly not achieved the objective the British had set for the assassination. Indeed one might have said it actually worked in favour of Germany. After the Lidice Massacre, the Germans had no further trouble with their Czech workers right up to the end of the war when the Third Reich was virtually defeated.

Skorzeny had extended irregular warfare into the area of such gangster methods as kidnapping and assassination of the enemies' high-ranking leaders. In the next two years Skorzeny and his Jagdkommando Friedenthal would be involved in operations against top enemy figures, such as Marshal Tito of Yugoslavia, Marshal Pétain of France, Admiral Horthy, dictator and ruler of Hungary, even the 'Big Three', Churchill, Stalin and Roosevelt.

As one of the three intended victims of the assassination planned for the Teheran Conference of November 1943, Winston Churchill declared during his account of the Mussolini rescue to the House of Commons: 'The stroke [the Skorzeny operation] was one of great daring and conducted with a heavy force. It certainly shows there are many possibilities of this kind open in modern warfare.'

Churchill was one of the Allied leaders who swiftly learned the lesson that Skorzeny had taught. Within the year two young British irregular soldiers would kidnap General Kneipe, commandant of German-occupied Crete and spirit him back to Allied lines. A few months after that, a Major William Fraser of the Gordon Highlanders, attached to the SAS, radioed SAS headquarters outside London: 'Very reliable source states Rommel's headquarters at Château de la Roche-Gyon. Rommel arrives left bank Seine, crosses by motor launch. Walks and shoots in Forêt de Moisson . . . [send] three snipers' rifles.'

Major Fraser's request was turned down by his commander, Brigadier R W McLeod, not because the latter had any qualms about using those three snipers' rifles on Germany's most senior commander in France, the 'Desert Fox', Marshal Rommel, but because 'this pigeon will be attacked by a special party'. A few days later, after studying the problem, McLeod issued Operation Instruction Number 32: 'Intention: To kill or kidnap and remove to England, Field Marshal Rommel.'

McLeod had, in theory, signed Rommel's death warrant. Once the SAS had pulled off the sensational coup of kidnapping Germany's senior commander in the West, it would have been virtually impossible for the SAS troopers to spirit the German out of France. That meant there was only one alternative left to them: <u>murder Rommel</u>!

*

While others outside Germany began planning operations on similar lines to the Mussolini rescue (including the OSS, the new American spy organisation and forerunner of the CIA), Skorzeny became sick of kicking his heels as a socialite in Berlin. He wanted to get back to his men. But before Hitler took leave of his new favourite, he gave Skorzeny the prize he was seeking: permission to recruit a special battalion for every front on which the Wehrmacht was currently engaged.

Once back in Friedenthal, Skorzeny had little time to oversee these new battalions of bold young men, seeking adventure in irregular warfare. Almost immediately he found himself deep into new plots. For a while he was sent to occupied France with the task of capturing a French national hero and current head of state, Marshal Pétain.

The aged soldier, who back in 1916 had been summoned from a Parisian brothel to save an almost defeated French Army, had come to an agreement with the German conquerors in 1940. It was almost as if he and the rest of those who ruled France's destiny at that time agreed with the then French Prime Minister's mistress, Comtesse de Portes, who stated, while her lover took to his bed: 'Since Hitler is the strongest, the best thing is to give in to him. *C'est tout.*' Even when the new British Prime Minister Churchill offered a union of Britain and France, in order to save Paris from the invading Germans, a French deputy shouted in disgust: 'Better be a Nazi province than a British dominion!'

Since 1940 France had been exactly that under Marshal Pétain's Vichy Government.* For two years after France's surrender, the Germans held a country of some 50 million citizens with a mere 30,000 troops. They didn't need more. The French were tame and the Pétain regime did most of Germany's dirty work for her. So diligent were the French in both the occupied and unoccupied parts of their country, that they even rounded up and handed over Jewish children to the Nazi torturers. In Paris, for instance, the resistance, mostly communist, numbered a mere 600 workers.

It was Skorzeny's task in France to ensure that Pétain didn't change sides when and if the Western Allies invaded his nation and was not spirited out of the country as the British had already succeeded in doing with two senior French officers (one of whom later became a marshal of France, though he had sworn back in '40, if the Germans needed his division in the invasion of Britain, he would gladly lead it against the *Rosbifs*). In the end that particular mission was called off and the aged 'Hero of Verdun' lived to be sentenced to exile as a traitor.

At the same time, while he was in France, Skorzeny built up a network of so-called 'sleepers'. These were men and women who, either because

*Named after the spa town of that name which was the seat of Pétain's government.

they were Nazi sympathisers or could be bought for hard currency – and Skorzeny now had plenty of that – were prepared to work for the Germans, even when and if the German occupiers were forced out of their country. Behind Allied lines, they would then report on the Allies' military movements and carry out acts of sabotage on their installations whenever possible. They and their like in Belgium and Holland were, as we will see, very useful to Skorzeny in his post-Allied invasion covert operations.

Hardly had the Pétain crisis been resolved than Skorzeny was rushed to Yugoslavia. Now the order given to him was 'Get Marshal Tito'. It was a mission very much to the scarfaced giant's liking, especially as the rest of the order stipulated, 'dead or alive'. The Yugoslav partisan leader had long interested him. The ex-sergeant-major in the Imperial Austrian Army had managed to weld together an outstanding partisan army in a country riddled with factions: pro-German Croatian forces fighting Serbian royalist partisans and all of the various political, religious and ethnic groupings waging war against one another. Skorzeny felt that if he could liquidate the mysterious Tito, he would contribute materially to the success of Germany's war effort. The partisan movement, which was the only one fighting directly against the Wehrmacht, would collapse and the thousands of German troops bogged down in wartorn Yugoslavia could be released to fight elsewhere, probably on the hard-pressed Russian front.

But the Tito mission didn't work out as Skorzeny thought it would. Although he risked his life travelling through partisan territory, armed solely with a sub-machine gun and accompanied by two NCOs of his Jagdkommando, an overzealous German corps commander, whose help he needed urgently, refused to cooperate with him.

So taking command personally, he launched a full-scale attack on Tito's HQ complete with parachutists and gliderborne troops. It was to be the Gran Sasso operation all over again: drop right on top of the objective, take enemy completely by surprise and deal with the key man, here Tito, on the spot. Just as he had done in his student duelling days, Skorzeny was going for the head.

Unfortunately, it didn't work out like that. Tito escaped from his cave HQ by the skin of his teeth, leaving Skorzeny possessor of the full marshal's uniform of which the self-appointed Field Marshal had been so proud. The partisan commander lived on to fight another day and become the head of a reunited Yugoslavia at the end of the war.

While all these varied 'political' missions were being embarked upon, not always to Skorzeny's satisfaction, his commandos of the Jagdkommando Friedenthal were carrying out much more sinister operations. After the war Skorzeny, vain and boastful as he was, decided it was wiser to draw a cloak of secrecy over them. As a prisoner of the Americans, he was what they called a 'hot number' and the scarfaced giant knew it. There were half a dozen countries in East and West who were after his hide and Skorzeny knew the '*Amis*' (i.e. the Americans) would hand him over as a war criminal, if he overstepped the mark. So he kept quiet about some of the more spectacular and politically dangerous ops in which he and his men had been involved.

There was 'Operation Long Jump' for example. This was the mission to assassinate the 'Big Three', Churchill, Stalin and Roosevelt, at the Teheran Conference of 1943. That November the three war leaders were to come together in the Persian capital to discuss the further conduct of the war.

Teheran was not exactly a safe place for the most powerful Allied leaders to meet, but it had been picked because Stalin, ever suspicious of other people's motives, including those of his allies, felt it was the closest to the Soviet Union and the Red Army bases in North Persia. For Skorzeny and his fellow plotters, on the other hand, it was an ideal place for them to wipe out the enemy leadership in one fell blow.

For months now the Germans had been dropping Persian-speaking officers, who had made contact with the mainly anti-British Persians, and had readily agreed to work for the Germans in return for a plentiful supply of what they called the 'Horsemen of St George' (gold sovereigns) and modern weapons.

Now as the Germans learned of the top level conference to be held in Teheran, they redoubled their efforts to infiltrate agents into Russia. This time, however, they were not to be used to raise the local tribes and stop the flow of Anglo-American weapons from the south of the country to the north where the Red Army was ready to receive them. These agents were coming as assassins and more deadly ones than their medieval Persian predecessors. The assassins of the Middle Ages, the secret Muslim order who, high on hashish, terrorised and murdered their Christian enemies, bore no comparison to these 20th-century killers who dropped by air and carried with them a deadly array of the most modern weapons.

But unfortunately for Skorzeny and his fellow plotters (and fortunately for the 'Big Three'), the Allies had already learned of the murder plot from their own agents in the Persian capital. There General Schwarzkopf (father of General 'Stormin' Norman' Schwarzkopf of Gulf War fame) and his British counterpart, Colonel Joseph Spencer, were ready for the German killers.

As Churchill's bodyguard, Inspector 'Tommy' Thompson later recalled:

> [on arrival] we started for the British Legation by the most unusual route. For security reasons, we travelled right across fields, secured beforehand for land mines. We were escorted by armoured cars. As we approached the centre of Teheran many of the people were out on the streets and on the street corners. Some got too close and got

knocked down. All entrances to the British Legation were guarded by troops. Many more troops were quartered in the grounds, but the measures were still not adequate.

Churchill himself, the object of the killers' intentions, didn't seem worried. As Thompson remembered: 'Winston had heard his life was threatened here. He was very excited, even pleased. He looked into everyone's face with the happiest sort of suspicion.'

Fortunately for Churchill, British security knew more of what to expect from Skorzeny's agents. The British had learned that the German agents were to be parachuted into Teheran in two drops. This would be done over two nights. On landing they were to be supplied by Persians on the ground with the latest details of Churchill's intended movements during the great conference.

On the first night Colonel Spencer 'nabbed the leader', as Thompson wrote, and 'let him set up shop at the point of rendezvous. In came the others, one by one, not knowing that there was a British gun trained on their leader. It was a good roundup, but we didn't get them all, so the tension remained.'

But Skorzeny's plan had been rumbled and although there were other scares in Teheran thereafter, the great scheme for bringing an immediate cessation of hostilities by assassinating the 'Big Three' had come to nought. Churchill, Roosevelt and Stalin returned to their respective countries unharmed, to bring about Germany's final defeat.

One of these many operations which did end successfully was forced on Skorzeny by Hitler's chief-of-operations, cunning-faced Colonel-General Jodl. It was 'one which it is specially important for the High Command to wash its hands of', as Major Radl, Skorzeny's adjutant, commented later.

In the late summer of 1943, when the German front in Russia had collapsed, nearly twenty-five German divisions had been torn apart or had surrendered. Many had not, although their divisional commanders had ordered them to do so. Thus it was, due to the stubbornness of a regimental commander, Lieutenant-Colonel Scherhorn, that remnants of a dozen regiments, some 2,000 men in all, still found themselves at liberty in the heart of Russia.

By the time Skorzeny was brought in to do something, Scherhorn and his men had been travelling westwards for nearly three months, bringing out their wounded with them. But their radio messages to the German High Command indicated that they were now becoming desperate, harassed as they were on all sides by Russian regulars and partisans. Despite their epic trek westwards, which had demanded the utmost of the ragged, half-starved column, they were about at the end of their tether. Something had to be done – and done soon. What could Skorzeny do?

Although this was not the kind of mission that the Viennese giant wanted to undertake (he wondered if Scherhorn really existed or was this a trap to lure him into Soviet hands?), he accepted the challenge. Hastily he assembled thirty volunteer commandos, whom he ordered not to shave, to smoke the horrible black tobacco the Russians smoked and dress in Russian uniform (which would mean they'd be shot on the spot as spies if the 'Ivans' caught them).* The volunteers would be parachuted into Russia by Skorzeny's own special air squadron (Squadron 200) to make the initial contact with Scherhorn's group, if it really existed.

Five hours later, Group A reported from the centre of Russia. 'Poor landing. Enemy have spotted us. We're under machine-gun fire.' That was the last that was heard of the volunteers.

Undeterred, Skorzeny dispatched Group B. For five days nothing was heard of Skorzeny's brave young men. Then on the night of the fifth day an excited clerk ran into Skorzeny's office, crying,' Obersturmbannführer . . . Obersturmbannführer, we've got them!' Not only had Group B landed safely, they had actually linked up with the mysterious Colonel Scherhorn and he was on the radio himself to express his thanks.

Thereafter Skorzeny faced innumerable difficulties. Indeed many of the High Command staff officers involved in the operation thought it was all a Soviet trick. Skorzeny persisted, however. He arranged for the trapped men to be supplied by air so that they could fight their way to some lakes near the city of Minsk. But planes were in short supply. In the end Skorzeny had fuel enough for only one plane. Berlin ordered the end of the operation.

With victory and rescue in sight, Scherhorn radioed Skorzeny: 'Where are the planes? Send to fetch us. We are running out of food.'

Skorzeny gave in reluctantly. He ordered the Knight's Cross to be dropped to Scherhorn, if it really was he. It was duly done and Scherhorn thanked the SS Colonel in one of the last radio messages received from the trapped men. Then silence.

Although the operation had to be counted as a failure, Skorzeny had learned something from it: another item that could be added to his collection of covert tricks. A handful of brave young men, dressed in the enemy's uniform and speaking the enemy's language, could be sent far behind the enemy's lines to carry out daring and exceedingly bold operations that a complacent enemy would not believe possible. It was something new that bore giving great thought and attention to. But before he could implement these new covert tricks, Skorzeny would be involved in one last political-military action that would change the face of the war in Central Europe.

*

*In a year's time Skorzeny would be dressing up other volunteers in foreign uniforms – this time *American*.

After the lost battle of Stalingrad and other subsequent German defeats, Hitler began to fear that his few allies in Eastern Europe would soon start to lose heart and defect to the triumphant Russians. In the summer of 1943 the Führer was already having trouble with Czar Boris, the ruler of Bulgaria.

While the wily Boris, the worthy son of his father, nicknamed 'Foxy Ferdinand' for his cunning ways, had entered the German bloc against the Russian communists, he had steadfastly refused to send Bulgarian soldiers against what he call 'my Slavic brothers'. By that summer Boris's attitude was changing rapidly, due perhaps to the influence of his wife, Czarina Giovanna. She was the daughter of King Victor Emmanuel of Italy, whose country was in the process of defecting from the so-called 'Pact of Steel'* and going over to the Western Allies.

In mid-August 1943 Boris was invited to visit Hitler at his mountain retreat in the German Alps, der Berghof. There Boris, tall, dark and handsome, found the Führer in 'a fit of incredible rage'. The meeting was a disaster; Boris still refused to send troops to Russia and Hitler obviously suspected that the Bulgarian Czar was about to enter secret negotiations with the enemy. In due course Boris flew back to the capital, Sofia, in a German plane, where his wife thought her husband 'looked very unwell as never before'. Eleven days after he had returned on 28 August, Boris fell into a coma and died.

Rumours soon started to circulate in Sofia that Boris had not died of natural causes. Rather he had been killed in some mysterious way by the Germans at Hitler's command. Popular speculation had it that the Czar had been somehow poisoned by the German pilot of his plane. The pilot had taken the aircraft up so high that Boris had been forced to use an oxygen mask. But instead of oxygen, the pilot had pumped some un-known poison gas down the tube which had led to the Czar's death.

As Boris lay dying, he had been examined by his German doctor, a Dr Seitz, plus two other German specialists flown in for the task. Together with the Czar's Bulgarian doctors, they issued a statement maintaining that Boris had died of a massive heart attack. Still the Bulgarian sceptics didn't believe the doctors. They declared as proof that their ruler had been a victim of an assassination the fact that no postmortem was carried out on Boris.**

And as that summer wore on, the rumours of a German plot persisted. Now, however, Hitler stepped in to blame his own enemies for Boris's sudden death. The Führer now maintained that the Czar's own wife had

*Composed of Italy, Japan and Germany.
**In fact, there was a secret one later. The verdict was the same as that of Boris's German doctors: Boris died of a massive heart attack.

killed her husband with the aid of her sister Princess Mafalda (she later died in Buchenwald concentration camp). They had poisoned the Czar. Later Hitler came up with another explanation of the strange death. He let it be known that he thought the Russians, with the aid of British Intelligence, had been instrumental in doing away with Boris.

Whatever the truth, it was clear that he now had to keep a wary eye on these members of the so-called 'Tripartite Pact'; for already some Bulgarians were beginning to negotiate secretly with the Russians. Thus it was that in that same early September, when a sick Hitler decided he would launch one last great surprise attack in the west (we shall hear more of this soon), Otto Skorzeny was summoned to spend the night at Hitler's HQ. There, after some desultory talk about the situation on the Eastern Front, the Führer got down to the reason for having summoned the head of the Jagdkommando. He told a shocked Skorzeny:

> We have secret information that the Hungarian Regent Admiral Horthy is attempting to make contact with the enemy to make a separate peace for Hungary. That would mean the loss of our armies [in Hungary]. Not only is he, Horthy, trying to negotiate with the Western Allies, he is also trying to arrange talks with the Russians.

Skorzeny understood what this would mean for Germany: she would lose a major ally and at the same time a great gap would be torn in the defences in the East.

'So Skorzeny,' Hitler continued, 'in case the Regent does not honour his pledges, you are to prepare for the military occupation of the Burgberg [Hitler meant the hill on which Horthy had his residence].'

Jodl now took up the briefing. Swiftly he sketched in the forces that were to be made available to Skorzeny for the daring operation. He'd be given a squadron of gliders, two parachute battalions and an elite formation made up of battle-hardened officer-cadets. In addition he was to receive a plane for his own private use. Finally Hitler handed him a document, adorned with the golden eagle of the Third Reich. It was signed by the Führer himself. It granted Skorzeny far-reaching powers which virtually overruled anyone, whatever his rank. In the end Hitler wished him good-bye, saying significantly, 'And remember Skorzeny, I'm relying on you.'

Three days later a certain 'Dr Wolf' from Cologne arrived in civilian clothes in the Hungarian capital. The scarfaced doctor took up residence in a modest hotel frequented by German officers, then sallied forth, a dog-eared Baedeker guide in his hand, to study the surroundings of the Burgberg (Castle Hill). Of course 'Dr Wolf' was Skorzeny, using (unwittingly) Hitler's old alias.

At the same time he tapped local German sources for what they knew about Admiral Horthy and his attitudes. The information was contradictory but all his German informants agreed that the old Admiral was slavishly devoted to his playboy youngest son, Miklos ('Miki') Horthy, notorious for his wild parties and the enfant terrible of the Regent's family. Still, since his oldest brother, Istvan, had been shot down as a pilot on the Russian front, 'Miki' could do no wrong in the eyes of his doting father.

In addition Skorzeny learned that Miki had already begun to negotiate with Tito, the Jugoslav partisan leader, and had agreed to surrender Hungary to the Russians, for whom Tito was working as an intermediary. Thus Skorzeny decided that the best way to put pressure on Horthy was to kidnap Miki with the aid of the local Gestapo. Operation 'Mickey Mouse' was born.

On Sunday 15 October 1944, the young Horthy was planning to meet the Yugoslav in the second-floor office of a house in the square near the River Danube. He didn't know it, but he was walking straight into Skorzeny's trap.

It was a quiet autumn Sunday morning in the Hungarian capital when Skorzeny drove into the square. The place was empty save for two Hungarian Army trucks parked outside the meeting place. A little farther on there was another canvas-back truck and a flash car which Skorzeny recognised as belonging to the playboy.

He parked and, opening the hood of his car, Skorzeny pretended to fiddle with the engine. An enquiring hand jerked back the canvas hood of the truck and Skorzeny was able to get a quick glimpse of a machine gun manned by three Hungarian soldiers before the hood fell back. The Hungarians were prepared for trouble.

But so was 'Dr Wolf'. Just about then two German 'chain dogs' (military policemen*) strolled up. Suddenly they lost their air of casual concern. Before anyone could stop them, they darted into the building where the meeting was being held. The Hungarians reacted. They jerked back the canvas and opened fire. A German MP slammed to the cobbles. Skorzeny darted forward. He pulled the wounded 'chain dog' into cover. Bullets spattered the length of his car like heavy tropical rain on a tin roof. The battle had commenced.

A group of Hungarian soldiers, who had been loitering in a nearby park, came rushing up with cries of help for their comrades manning the machine gun. Skorzeny's driver was hit. He went down groaning as Germans from his Jagdkommando under Captain von Voelkersam came running up firing from the hip.

The sight of the big tough commandoes took the heart out of the

---

*So called on account of the silver plate attached to a chain they wore around their necks as a badge of office.

Hungarians. They fled. But in the house the Hungarians were still prepared to fight on. As Skorzeny's commandos advanced, throwing stick grenades, the Hungarians on the upper floor retaliated by dropping bricks, marble slabs and heavy pieces of concrete on to them. Here and there Skorzeny's men fell to the ground, knocked unconscious by the unusual missiles.

Under Skorzeny's command, the rest bolted into the house, working their way to the upper floor where members of the Gestapo had already seized Miki. But Horthy's favourite son was not taking his arrest calmly. He was shouting and waving his arms wildly, as he threatened his captors with dire penalties as soon as he was released.

Skorzeny had no time to play games with the spoilt playboy. His eyes fell on a large, flowered carpet. Not far off was a curtain rope, a thick piece of tassel. He didn't hesitate. Swiftly he rapped out an order. Without ceremony Miki was wrestled to the floor. In vain he struggled with his captors. The carpet was wrapped around him. In an instant he was strapped in with the aid of the curtain rope.

Knowing that time was of the essence and that soon the whole of Budapest would be alerted. Skorzeny yelled above the snap and crackle of small arms fire outside: 'To the airfield'. 'I'll follow.' Then he added to von Voelkersam, 'No more shooting, *verstehen*?'

The whole action had taken less than ten minutes. Now Skorzeny had his hostage. How would the old Admiral, who had once served in the Austro-Hungarian Imperial Fleet, react? Impatiently Skorzeny waited for news. It was disappointing. The Horthy residence had been sealed off. Mines had been laid on the approach roads. Did that mean a fight? An hour later Horthy went on Budapest Radio to confirm that it might well be the case.

Angrily he denounced the Germans, his allies. The Germans had lost the war, Horthy declared firmly. Hungary must draw its own conclusions. He ended his broadcast with the admission that he had already drawn up a provisional armistice with the advancing Red Army. However, with typical Hungarian carelessness, his staff had forgotten to inform the Hungarian Army. Consequently their officers and men were still resisting the Russian invaders.

That news gave Skorzeny new hope, Hastily he drew up another plan, which became known as *Unternehmen Panzerfaust* (Operation Rocket Launcher). It envisaged the storming of Horthy's residence, Castle Hill. The leisurely approach of the German 22nd Division would, he hoped, indicate to the Hungarian defenders that the Germans were preparing for a lengthy siege of the hill. Then at dawn, a couple of sorties would be launched against the Hungarians to distract their attention. In the meantime the Skorzeny commandos would slip up one of the roads, the men sitting at attention in the backs of their vehicles to fool the Hungarians into not firing;

they were intended to think the unsuspecting Germans had not heard of the armistice and were on a routine road march.

Now, as was often the case with Skorzeny, fortune played into his hands. That evening, as he worked feverishly at his plan, a Hungarian general stormed into Skorzeny's HQ. He protested at the appearance of the 22nd SS Division on the Burgberg. What were the Germans up to? Skorzeny retaliated quickly. He demanded to know why German diplomats were being confined to their quarters on the hill. What were the Hungarians going to do with them?

The general flushed with shame. He felt the honour of Hungary was being attacked. Skorzeny took advantage of the Hungarian's embarrassment. He suggested that all the mines and barriers should be removed from the Wienerstrasse which led up to the German diplomats' quarters. The Hungarian general said he'd see what he could do.

At six that morning, Skorzeny set off on his dangerous mission. Behind him he had four tanks in his column, a troop of 'Goliath' tanks, a remote-controlled mini-panzer filled with high explosive, and truckload after truckload of infantry. Soon the tense soldiers started to relax. Their way was not barred. The Hungarian general had had the mines and obstacles removed. Here and there a few shots were fired, but Skorzeny managed to penetrate the castle easily.

Striding masterfully inside he knocked on a great door. It was opened by a Hungarian major-general. 'Are you the commandant of the Burgberg?' he asked. The Hungarian said he was. Skorzeny shouted for effect, 'I demand you surrender the Burgberg at once! You are responsible if any more blood is spilled. I ask you for an immediate decision.'

The Hungarian complied. The two men shook hands and once again Skorzeny had pulled it off. For some reason the Viennese giant remembered that Hungary had once been an integral part of the Austro-Hungarian Empire until 1918. So putting on his best Austrian accent, he told the assembled Hungarian officers:

> I would like to remind you that for centuries Hungarians have never fought against Austrians. Always we have been allies. Now there is no reason for difficulties . . . our concern is the new Europe. But this can only be achieved if Germany survives.

Skorzeny, unwittingly, was using the new concept created by the 'Poison Dwarf', Dr Goebbels, Minister of Propaganda: that they were all fighting the 'Reds' to help create a new Europe. Naturally Germany would lead that 'new Europe'. But as Skorzeny remembered: 'My Austrian accent obviously supported and strengthened my words, something which I felt in the pressure of their hands when I shook hands with each of them afterwards.'

Unternehmen Panzerfaust was over at the cost of less than twenty German casualties. Admiral Horthy was removed from his residence and immediately sent to Germany by special train as 'guest of the Führer'. His abdication as Regent was announced shortly afterwards. In his place, the new German-Hungarian appointed Count Szalasi, who was pro-German, immediately withdrew from the armistice that Horthy had drawn up with the Russians.

Thus Hungary remained Germany's ally, the only one Hitler had left in Europe, with Count Szalasi continuing the fight against the 'Reds', even when his capital, Budapest, was surrounded by the Red Army in mid-December 1944.

Otto Skorzeny, for his part, had in the meantime taken up residence in the palace, enjoying life like 'the King in France', as the Germans say. He drank champagne and probably enjoyed the services of willing Hungarian beauties (the Austrian giant was a bit of a ladies' man; it was said after the war that he became the lover of Eva Peron when he was in exile in Argentina) and bathed every day in the baroque bath-tub once owned by the aged Austrian-Hungarian Emperor of his youth, Kaiser Franz-Josef.

Hitler had personally ordered Skorzeny to have a few days' rest. He said he deserved it. Again the head of Jagdkommando Friedenthal had pulled off a tremendous coup. He'd kept Hungary in the war and had saved the whole of the German central front from collapsing due to a defection of the Hungarian Army.

But his time out of the war was going to be of short duration. Already new tasks were awaiting Otto Skorzeny. In the last year or so, he had changed the war in Italy, done the same in Hungary, and had attempted to do likewise in Teheran with the assassination of the 'Big Three'. Now the ailing Führer had a mission for him in the West. If Skorzeny succeeded this time, it might well be that he would completely transform the war in the West. Not only might his efforts help to ease the almost unbearable pressure on Germany on the Western Front, they could lead, if successful, to a compromise peace with the Anglo-Americans that would leave Hitler to deal with the hated Russians once and for all.

Book Two

Kill Ike

'When the disproportion of Power is so great that no limitation of our own object can ensure us safety from catastrophe forces will, or should, be concentrated in one desperate blow'.

Carl von Clausewitz: *On War*

CHAPTER I

Where is the Supreme Commander?

In the winter of 1944, all the talk was of murder and political assassination. Both in the Anglo-American camp and that of the German enemy, the unspoken truce of 1939 had been breached time and time again. Now the liquidation of political enemies had become policy, which was discussed at the highest level and not left to thugs such as Naujocks (now deserted to the Allies) and poor dead foreign assassins such as Gabcik and Kubis.

Back in 1940 Mussolini had joked that the US Secret Service was 'the best in the world because no one knows where it is'. In other words, an American secret service didn't exist.* One year later, just as the USA was entering the war, President Roosevelt asked 'Wild Bill' Donovan, a much decorated veteran of WWI, to form one, telling the corporate lawyer somewhat gloomily: 'Bill, you will have to begin with nothing. We have *no* intelligence service.'

Major-General Donovan, as he now was, a New York Irishman, who was one of only three US soldiers who held all three tops decorations for bravery, including the Congressional Medal of Honor, was undaunted. With all his formidable energy, he set about the task of forming an organisation from scratch which became known later as the Office of Strategic Services – the OSS.

Scholars and adventurers, crooks and cops, secret Russian spies and 'commie-haters', men and women of half a dozen national backgrounds, rallied to Donovan's new outfit almost immediately. Some were out for an unorthodox war, others sought a 'quick buck' or safe billet for the duration. A lot were talented men and women, who knew Europe well, and felt they could best use their particular gifts in the pursuit of victory under Wild Bill's command.

At first, however, the OSS was plagued with dead-beats and undesirables. There were academics who believed their PhDs qualified them for a desk job and at least the rank of major. There were crackpot inventors who

---

*There *was* an American Secret Service, but its function was not to collect foreign intelligence, but to look after the President and, to some extent, the affairs of the US Treasury.

created 'explosive bread' which could be eaten if the agent felt he was under suspicion – though it wasn't thought advisable to smoke a cigarette immediately afterwards – or a loathsome chemical nicknamed 'who me'. It duplicated the smell and consistency of a loose bowel movement. Its purpose, according to its inventor, was to be sprayed on the breeches of high-ranking Japanese officers so that they would lose 'face' in front of the 'natives'.

It was not surprising therefore, that by 1942 when Donovan's organisation was really getting underway, he was still being mocked by the capital's press as 'Hush-Hush Bill', while his outfit, filled with Ivy League graduates and members of the US Social Register such as the Duponts, Vanderbilts, Roosevelts and the like, was made fun of on the Washington cocktail circuit as 'oh, so silly' or even worse 'organisation shush-shush'.

Even the Germans seemed to have picked up details of Wild Bill's group, which now combined the functions of the British SIS and SOE, and commented in their radio broadcasts beamed at the USA that it consisted of 'fifty professors, twenty monkeys, ten goats, twenty guinea-pigs – and a staff of Jewish scribblers'. The reference to the animals in the German broadcast was explained by the fact that Donovan had had to locate some of his officers and their sections in the Washington National Health Institute, where they shared quarters with the latter's experimental labs.

In the spring of 1942, when the main body of the OSS had moved to London under the command of an Ivy Leaguer, Colonel David Bruce, things changed somewhat. Those who had survived the Washington weeding-out process now found themselves confronted with the grim and vicious realities of their new profession. The days of the cocktail circuit, the brittle, classy chat about the cosmos and the fancy tailor-made uniforms were over. English SOE went to work on them. They went through the usual tough commando training, and although this was only training, they could guess what the real thing would entail. The bent backs, the missing fingernails, the scarred faces of their SOE instructors spoke eloquently of what happened to an agent in Occupied Europe who missed and fell into the hands of the Gestapo.

By 1944 the OSS had 30,000 agents operating all over the world and unlimited 'slush funds' at its disposal. Now the 'Yanks' started to inject a fresh approach to clandestine operations against the German enemy. It was neither sophisticated nor subtle. The leadership of the OSS in London and Washington wanted their agents to conduct a no-holds-barred, covert battle against the Nazis. Spying and sabotage would now have to take second place to direct and violent action in Europe.

Using a kind of early mobile phone which could communicate between an agent on the ground and a pilot in a plane flying high above, the OSS 'Jedburgh teams' could transmit information directly to and from their airborne comrades. This put an end to the old-fashioned, long-winded business of radio operators, hidden in some garret, trying to get through in code to London, passing on information that might well be out-of-date by the time it was translated into 'clear'.

Dangerous as the 'Jedburgh' operations were, they were already in place in France and Belgium by the time of D-Day. British SIS and SOE agents on the ground were horrified by the Americans' disregard for their own lives and those of the Continental agents. Time and time again, the OSS teams ran operations, especially in the south of France, which resulted in large-scale and vicious reprisals by the SS and their French fascist police accomplices, the Milice.

But although the OSS 'new boys' were mainly concerned that summer with preventing German reinforcements from the south of France reaching the D-day beaches, they were also actively engaged in plans to assassinate top-ranking Germans. Reportedly it was an OSS agent who tipped off the Allies where Rommel's headquarters were. Thereafter, what might be termed an 'aerial ambush' was set up. In July 1944 a lone British Spitfire attacked the Desert Fox's staff car as it ran down a lonely French coast road. The commander of all the German troops in Normandy was gravely wounded in the attack. The wound took him out of the war and, incidentally, out of the German generals' plot to assassinate Hitler on the 22nd of that same month.

Naturally the OSS considered murdering Hitler and the 'mad professor'. Dr Lovell, the inventor of many of the OSS's gadgets, came up with several weird and wonderful devices to be used in the attempt. But there were those in the OSS, especially working with Allen Dulles, a future head of the CIA, right-wing capitalists with pre-war connections to German banking and business, who hesitated to advocate the murder of the Führer, unless the Germans did it themselves. They didn't want to make a martyr of Hitler, with the German people maintaining after the war and an Allied victory that Germany had been stabbed in the back again, just as the Fatherland had been in 1918.

Besides, the Dulles group feared what might happen to a Germany that had suddenly had its guiding light taken away from it. Would it go over to the communists who were now coming in from the east? What would happen to their investments and plans for an americanised big business then? For already the Dulles group were talking to representatives of German business at their base in supposedly neutral Switzerland. Soon they'd even be negotiating with Himmler's SS generals. As one of these elegant, pre-war American lawyers now masquerading as OSS agents told little homosexual British SOE operative Denis Rake, who had been in and out of Occupied Europe several times during the pre-D-Day period: 'We're one-dollar-a-year men, you know.' He meant he and his fellow upper crust agents were accepting only nominal pay. Later Rake commented caustically: 'One dollar a day! Blimey, that's exactly what they're worth!'

The problem of what might happen in Germany following a successful assassination of the Führer plagued the British planners of what became known as 'Operation Foxley', which was also being worked out in the summer of 1944. 'Foxley' envisaged an attempt on Hitler's life and it had been provisionally sanctioned by Churchill. For now the gloves were off. After two alleged attacks on his own life, Churchill was not disinclined to see the Führer 'bumped off', as he put it.

Naturally the two secret organisations involved in 'Foxley' accepted Churchill's decisions. But the SIS under General Menzies, who was closer to the Foreign Office (nominally the SIS came under the command of the Foreign Office), was a little hesitant about going ahead with the plan of assassination. The SOE, in particular 'X Section', under the command of hard-bitten, tough General Gerald Templer, who had been badly wounded as a divisional commander in Italy and then transferred to the SOE, was all for the plan.

Templer, code-named AD/X, worked hard to find a suitable means of 'sending Hitler to hell', as he was quoted as saying. His German Division worked with the other technical branches of the SOE, not only to find out the details of the Führer's movements, but also to discover the most suitable way of dispatching him. These included poisoned tea – the SOE researchers naturally didn't know that all the Führer's food was tasted before he consumed it, an aerial bombardment of the Berghof at Berchtesgaden in the Bavarian Alps, and a lone sniper. There was also the derailment of Hitler's personal train between Salzburg and Berchtesgaden, the poisoning of the train's water supply, and a bomb in a suitcase thrown beneath the train as it slowed down to enter Berchtesgaden Station.

In the most part these plans were unworkable. How would the British smuggle in agents to carry out the deed when the Berchtesgaden area was guarded by SS and Alpine troops and the whole place had been made into a *Sperrgebiet*, a restricted area, for the local Bavarian peasant farmers? Still the murder plan was given clearance by the Foreign Secretary Anthony Eden (in later years Eden would plan to have Nasser of Egypt murdered too) and Churchill was now informed of what was afoot.

But by the winter of 1944, the SOE, which had been given the task of carrying out the assassination with the aid of the SIS, was split on the value of the operation. Gubbins, the SOE head, and Templer were for it. As Air Vice Marshal A P Ritchie of the organisation expressed their attitude, Hitler was regarded by most Germans 'as something more than human'.

'It is this mystical hold which he exercises over the German people that is largely responsible for keeping the country together at the present time,' Ritchie said. 'Remove Hitler and there is nothing left.'

Others were sceptical. 'As a strategist Hitler has been of the greatest possible assistance to the British war effort,' an SOE officer, Major Field-Robertson, wrote, referring to Hitler's strategic blunders during the war. 'I have no hesitation in saying that his value to us has been the equivalent to an almost unlimited number of first class SOE agents strategically placed inside Germany.'

So the arguments raged back and forth inside the Intelligence community until finally in November 1944, 'Operation Foxley' was put on a kind of permanent hold, though five months later one really determined attempt *was* made to assassinate the Führer when he was believed to have taken refuge in Berchtesgaden in what American Intelligence was by then calling the 'Mountain Fastness',* the site of the Nazis' last stand. It failed, too, for the man who had escaped assassination time and time again, did the job himself in the end. He shot himself in his bunker in Berlin.

In Germany, too, detailed planning was taking place that November for a series of assassinations to be carried out behind Allied lines. This time, however, the targets were to be not enemy politicians or leaders, but the plotters' fellow Germans, who had volunteered to work with the Allied occupiers.

That month Skorzeny was called away from his own planning at Friedenthal to report to Himmler's HQ at Hohenlychen near Berlin. He was received by Himmler personally. With him the Reichsführer SS had a cohort of the highest ranked police, Gestapo and Intelligence officers in the SS. There was General Schellenberg, of course, who in what now seemed another age had organised the kidnapping of Best and Stevens. There was another Austrian giant there too, scarfaced Doktor Kaltenbrunner, who had replaced Heydrich and whose breath smelled so badly that Himmler himself had ordered him to go to a dentist immediately. And there was 'Gestapo' Mueller, the man who had interrogated the two captured British agents and who was the least known of all the Nazi police *Prominenz.***

Himmler – naturally – opened the meeting himself with one of his customary long-winded introductions before turning to Skorzeny and saying: 'I want you to take over the Werewolf organisation and knock it

---

*Later known as the 'Mountain Redoubt'.
**Mueller stayed in Berlin after the collapse of the Third Reich. When his supposed grave was dug up in the summer of 1945 it was found to contain the bones of three other men. Some historians of the Third Reich maintain that he survived to flee to the USA where he worked for the CIA until his death.

into shape.' Before Skorzeny had time to react, Himmler launched into a detailed account of what this new secret organisation he had just set up would do.

The 'Werewolf', named after the mythical, medieval creature which could transform itself from a human being into a rampaging wolf, had been born in the first week of November 1944 when, carried away by his own eloquence during a speech to the new Volksturm (the German Home Guard), Himmler had declared that soon loyal Germans would be able to strike the rear, the enemy-occupied German territories, 'coming and going like wolves'.

In essence, brave young German men and women, most of them teenagers, would carry out acts of sabotage and assassination behind Allied lines, dealing with those traitors who co-operated with the Anglo-Americans. Schellenberg had protested to his boss Himmler that the idea 'was madness'. But in the end he had been won over and was now busy recruiting some 5,000 males and females for operations in enemy territory.

Already Schellenberg had set up secret arsenals, guarded by young volunteers, many of them adventurous teenagers, who had been formed into cells with secret words and all the trappings of clandestine operations. Now these youngsters from the Hitler Youth and Hitler Maidens were beginning 'to consider it our supreme duty to kill, to kill and to kill, employing,' as Radio Werewolf proclaimed, 'every cunning, and while in the darkness of night, crawling, groping through towns and villages, like wolves, noiselessly, mysteriously'.

Now Himmler wanted Skorzeny to take over this new outfit. For, as Himmler said, hadn't he already set up his own 'sleeper' organisation of French, Belgians, Dutch and the like behind Allied lines who were waiting for his, Skorzeny's, call to arms? Skorzeny agreed with the Reichsführer, but he didn't tell Himmler that he was already preparing to use those 'sleepers' for missions which were far more important than the assassination of some traitor who had become the burgomaster of some Godawful Eifel village, now occupied by the Amis.

Himmler must have seen the look of doubt on Skorzeny's scarred face, which looked as it it was the work of some crazy butcher's apprentice, for as he said after a moment: 'I know, Skorzeny, this job would fall into your competence, but I think you've got enough on at the moment.'

Skorzeny agreed quickly. 'Certainly, Reichsführer, I've more than enough to do. But I'd like to make a suggestion . . . I take over all operations [of this kind] *outside* the borders of the Reich.'

Himmler nodded his approval and Skorzeny concealed his delight. He didn't want a bunch of crazy schoolkids in short pants getting in the way of his own great clandestine operation in the Low Countries and France. As Skorzeny wrote later in his memoirs:

I pointed out the senselessness of the Werewolf organisation which was being forced to carry on the struggle . . . This plan, I said to Himmler, would bring nothing but suffering to the German people. Opportunities would arise for every sort of crime to be committed.

According to Skorzeny after the war, Himmler waved away his objections, *if* Skorzeny ever made them. For by now his own secret plans embraced missions that would give rise 'for every sort of crime to be committed . . .'.

For Skorzeny it had all started two months earlier on 21 October, when he had been ordered to attend the Führer at his HQ *die Wolfsschanze* (the Wolf's Lair). In spite of enfeebled health, Hitler received the head of the Jagdkommando with a firm handshake, clasping Skorzeny's big hand with both of his. 'Well done, Skorzeny,' he greeted the other man warmly. 'Now tell me about this operation – "Mickey Mouse".' He meant the kidnapping of Admiral Horthy's favourite son.

Skorzeny told the story of his Hungarian mission in detail, only interrupted by Hitler's laughter when he explained how he had wrapped the young playboy in the flowered carper. Then, when he had finished, Skorzeny rose to go.

But Hitler detained him. 'Stay a while,' he suggested, his sallow, yellow face, the result of jaundice, flushed a little, 'I am now going to give you the most important job of your life. In December Germany will start a great offensive. It may decide her fate.

The statement made Skorzeny sit up and he listened attentively as Hitler explained how the Allies expected to find a 'stinking corpse' in Germany. However, they were in for a surprise. The Allies had won the 'battle of the invasion' only because they had possessed absolute air superiority. But that would all change. For his new offensive, Hitler explained, he had picked a period when the weather would be on Germany's side: overcast skies, snow and fog. That would deter the Allied planes. In addition, Hitler said: 'We will employ two thousand of the new jet fighters we have kept in reserve for the offensive.'

Skorzeny was impressed as Hitler went on to say that his offensive was aimed at preventing the recruitment of a new and powerful French Army and that would mean the Allies' planned attack to the Rhine would be postponed for months. In the meantime, his own army would push through the thinly held American front in the Eifel–Ardennes to the Meuse river. From here his tanks would race for the key supply port of Antwerp and drive a wedge between the Americans and the British.

Hitler then mused that the British and Americans were already beginning to fall out. They were at loggerheads over the question of

Greece and the civil war raging there. It appeared that the Amis had refused to supply ships to carry British troops to Greece to stop the civil war. If he, Hitler, could push the Western Allies back to the coast and perhaps knock Britain out of the war for good, he might be able to deal with Russia by battle or negotiation (he was already having secret talks with Russian representatives). Hitler paused and then explained:

> I have told you so much so that you will realise that everything has been considered very carefully and has been well worked out ... Now you and your units will play a very important role in this offensive. As an advance guard you will capture one or more bridges over the River Meuse between Liège and Namur. You will carry out this operation in British or American uniforms. The enemy has already used this trick. Only a couple of days ago, I received the news that Americans had worn German uniforms during their operations in Aachen.

He took a breather while Skorzeny tried to take in all the new information and remember the geographical details of this great new offensive without reference to notes or maps. Hitler went on:

> I know you'll do your best. But now to the most important thing. Absolute secrecy. Only a few people know of the plan. In order to conceal your preparations from your own troops, tell them we are expecting a full-scale enemy attack between Cologne and Bonn. Your preparations are intended to be part of the resistance to that attack.

Skorzeny mentioned that time was short and Hitler agreed. He finished with a friendly warning: 'But one thing, Skorzeny. I do not want you to cross the front line personally. You must not run the risk of being captured.' Skorzeny accepted the warning and was then passed on to Jodl and Field Marshal Keitel, Hitler's wooden-headed chief-of-staff, for further briefings. There Skorzeny's own personal account of what happened that October day ended.

Later when he came to write his own story in the 1950s, there were no other survivors of that meeting with Hitler and the subsequent briefing. Hitler had committed suicide and both Jodl and Keitel had been executed as war criminals. So, as no transcripts were made of this conversation between Hitler and Skorzeny, sitting side-by-side on Hitler's sofa, we are left with only Skorzeny's account of the details. One must, therefore, ask did Skorzeny tell the truth, even some five years after the war had ended and he was a free man again? For he had just escaped being extradited as a war criminal, thanks to his American protectors and in the east there were several states, including Soviet Russia, which wanted to bring him to justice for alleged war crimes.*

What then would Skorzeny have to hide? That final warning, as Skorzeny spells it out, that he must not go beyond the front line in the coming fighting gives a first clue that the Viennese giant was attempting to hide something. Hitler might have liked Skorzeny a great deal, just as he liked other bold, dashing SS officers, such as Obersturmbannführer Peiper, who would lead the attack of the 6th SS Panzer Army. But the Führer was not in the habit of warning them not to venture into enemy territory. Skorzeny himself, as we have seen, had risked his own neck several times behind the enemy front. Why then this warning from the Führer himself now?

We can only assume that Hitler didn't issue any warning to Skorzeny. Indeed it was part of the alibi that the head of the Jagdkommando prepared for himself once he had been captured by the Americans. If he couldn't cross the front line into territory held by the Amis during the battle to come, then he could in no way be associated with any crime carried out there by his men.

As we have seen, Hitler felt that if his counter-attack was successful he would be able to drive a wedge between the Anglo-American Allies. With luck Britain might be knocked out of the fighting war for a while; she was scraping the barrel for soldiers as it was. But the coalition between the US and British politicians and military would be restored sooner or later, if Eisenhower remained in his post as Supreme Commander.

By now Hitler had realised that the Americans had become the dominant force in the military alliance in North-West Europe. That November America was fielding three soldiers for every British one. Since 1942 the American and British roles had been reversed. The one-time junior partner, the US military, had now become the senior. And the man who had made it possible for the British, in particular their Prime Minister Winston Churchill, to accept their new role as junior partner was General Eisenhower. With his broad, ear-to-ear grin, his charm and political skills unusual in a professional soldier, the American general, who had come to London in 1942 as a complete unknown, had weathered many storms and difficulties within the military coalition.

But what if Eisenhower were removed? How would the Western Allies fare if, after a major military defeat, there was no 'Ike' to weld their shattered and probably demoralised armies together again? Who would – could – take his place? It couldn't be an Englishman such as Montgomery

---

*The author learned, after he had interviewed a sick Skorzeny in the late '60s, that he had been trailed by probably Czech Intelligence. All those years later, the Czechs and other states in the Eastern bloc were still interested in what Eisenhower would call 'the most dangerous man in Europe'.

who was heartily detested by most of the senior American generals. 'The little fart', as Patton routinely called him, had blotted his copybook far too often as far as the Americans were concerned. Not even Field Marshal Alexander could take over command. Lazy as the handsome guardsman was, he was still very popular with his American soldiers. All the same he was an Englishman, too, a junior partner.

What American could take over, Hitler must have reasoned. Who had the political and military skills needed to restore the fighting efficiency of the shaken coalition after a defeat in the field of battle? Certainly not Bradley, the American ground commander. The British had no confidence in him. Churchill had called him a 'surly, miserable bugger'. Although he had advanced up the ladder of promotion swiftly in the last four years, Bradley was not well liked in Washington. The President, the Commander-in-Chief of the American forces, knew little of him and General Marshall, Roosevelt's chief-of-staff, would have felt that Bradley would have been out of his depth in command in Europe. After all, the lantern-jawed, bespectacled Bradley had been a teacher of maths at West Point for most of his pre-war career.

What about General Marshall himself? He had once coveted the post of Supreme Commander. Unlikely. He was too old. He didn't know the personalities in Europe well enough and the austere general, who wouldn't even allow the President to call him by his first name, wouldn't have been a suitable candidate for someone like Churchill, who often behaved like an overgrown schoolboy. As for General MacArthur, a real fighting soldier, he reigned as a virtual dictator in the Pacific. He wouldn't want to give up all that power to come to Europe with everyone, as MacArthur would see it, peering over his shoulder and telling him what to do.

It could well have seemed to Hitler, who at the beginning of the war had agreed to the unspoken truce that political opponents should not be removed by assassination, that the murder of the American Supreme Commander would be a major factor in keeping the Western Allies out of Germany until 1945 – and by then many things might have swung in Germany's favour. The assassination of General Eisenhower would not be a military assassination but a political one.

And who else to carry out political assassination or kidnapping but Skorzeny, who in the last year and a half had carried out several such operations. Three times his fellow Austrian had achieved a major success in this area. Besides the operation behind enemy lines, *Unternehmen Greif* ('Operation Grab'), which he had suggested to Skorzeny, would surely not be enough for the commando, with his far-reaching ideas. In essence the mission he had originally offered Skorzeny that October day consisted of two things: sabotage and spying operations behind enemy lines; and the use of Skorzeny's new 150 Panzer Brigade to lead the way for Dietrich's 6th SS Panzer Army to the Meuse.

Would such a role satisfy the scarfaced giant? Vain and arrogant as Skorzeny had become, elevated from the sick list as an SS captain to a colonel, who had been informed of the coming offensive before most of the generals who would command Hitler's armies, cops and divisions in the counter-offensive, how would he take to this relatively subordinate action? There would be no high awards or honours to be won in a covert action such as 'Operation Grab'.

On the basis of Skorzeny's past record of top-level achievements, it was obvious that he would not be pleased with a subordinate role. The head of the Jagdkommando would have wanted more. Greedy for glory and the headlines which had followed his daring rescue of Mussolini (why even Churchill had praised him in the House of Commons!), Skorzeny would not have hesitated for a moment if Hitler had ordered him to assassinate Eisenhower. Just like the men that Skorzeny would soon be sending to their deaths (on account of that fact that they would be engaged in combat behind enemy lines, dressed in enemy uniform, and therefore could be shot as spies), he would be prepared to risk his life if he could bring off a coup that would make his name throughout the world.

The question that October now remained where exactly was the intended victim, Dwight D Eisenhower, Supreme Commander and future President of the United States, the most powerful man in the world?

Four years before Skorzeny's fateful meeting with Hitler on the evening of Friday 28 June 1940, a long line of lorries, pushcarts, and horse-drawn carts were drawn up at the White Rock Quay, Guernsey in the British Channel Islands. Their owners, farmers and market-gardeners, were preparing to unload their 'chips' – twelve pound baskets of tomatoes – into the holds of waiting British freighters. The tomatoes were intended for the British market. It was a fine evening and the locals chatted among themselves in their French patois. Over the water on the continent the war was raging, but here on the islands all that seemed a very long way off.

Then, suddenly, startlingly, at five to seven, six planes flashed overhead. They came from the east, gathering speed by the second. The locals, caught by surprise, shaded their eyes against the setting sun, wondering what the devil was going on. Above them three of the strange planes raced right across the island from east to west. The other three started to lose height swiftly. They were coming down. An instant later someone spotted the cross and swastika on the lead plane's fuselage. 'Jerries!' he yelled, using the English word for the Germans.

A moment later, the machine guns began to chatter angrily. The locals panicked. Some threw themselves down under their vehicles, as their horses reared and snorted with fear. Others dropped beneath the pier, and pressed their faces to the shingle. A few were terrified enough to jump into the water.

Almost before the local gardeners and farmers were aware of what was happening, the German planes were vanishing, roaring into the evening sky. Behind them they left a sorry mess of dead and dying civilians, their blood mingling with the squashed red pulp of Guernsey's pride, their tomatoes. The Germans had arrived in the Channel Islands, the only part of the British Empire that they would occupy in WWII.

Four years of German occupation followed. They were hard years. In this one-time holiday island which had been a place of plenty, foodstuffs became ever harder to obtain. By 1944 that British staple, tea, cost £28 a pound and an ordinary bar of soap ten shillings. Still the islanders had their cricket and football, as of old, complete with 'fixtures' against their enemies, the Germans.

There were dances, too, behind locked doors, the music of the forbidden BBC. And it wasn't only the male islanders who attended; the 'Jerries' did, too. They weren't short of female partners either. There were plenty of 'Jerry bags' who would dance with them – and more. By 1942 with the numbers of illegitimate children rising – and VD too – the German authorities had to issue an order stating: 'Sexual relations with either German soldiers or civilians are strictly forbidden for the next three months.' But apparently the amorous Germans and their island paramours couldn't wait that long; the rate of VD continued to rise.

By June 1944, when the Allies had just landed on the Continent, the food situation on the island had become very bad. And that of their 30,000 occupiers of the 'Division Kanada' as they called themselves (because they thought they'd end the war now as POWs in Canada) was little better. Their rations were cut to 1,125 calories a day, not much more than that of the prisoners in their concentration camps. TB was an epidemic among the troops. Military doctors estimated that only five per cent of 'Division Kanada' were fit for combat.

Despite the poor condition of the troops, their commanders on the island were still determined to fight, even now when the islands were cut off from the continental mainland. As a result the mutinous troops formed secret societies which were even prepared to assassinate their officers if they didn't soon give in to the Allied demands for surrender.

But there was one seemingly insurmountable problem facing these would-be mutineers, eager to surrender. It was the 'Madman of the Channel Islands', as they called him behind his back. He was 46-year-old Admiral Huffmeier, the one-time commandant of the German battleship *Scharnhorst* and now naval commander of the forces in this occupied territory.

Tall and hard-boiled, Huffmeier was a fervent Nazi. He didn't believe that he and his command should play a passive role now that they had been cut off. Once the Bailiff of Jersey, Alexander Coutanchea, said to Huffmeier: 'In truth, Admiral, both you and I are prisoners of the British Royal Navy.' Huffmeier's answer was a cynical, 'That's what you think,

Bailiff.' For Huffmeier felt, if necessary, he'd send his ragged, hungry 'Division Kanada' to fight in France.

Thus it was that Huffmeier started to collect whatever information he could about enemy troops, basically American, on the other side of the Channel, with an eye to using it for whenever he 'attacked'. But as the Western Allies captured one port after another along the French coast in Normandy and Brittany, the pressure on the Nazi Admiral mounted. Churchill, who was not prepared to waste precious troops on trying to capture the occupied British territory, ordered that no German should be allowed to escape from the islands and no food sent in. The Americans, on the other hand, wanted to see the end of the occupation of the Channel Islands. They were too close to their newly captured ports and at that time, with their future main supply port, Antwerp, still in German hands, they needed all these French harbours from Cherbourg southwards. Accordingly they attempted to get the cut-off Germans to surrender.

On 9 September 1944 an American plane flew across Guernsey, dropping flares instead of the expected bombs, as if to advise the Germans below of its presence. By the ruddy lights of these flares, which the Germans called 'Christmas trees', the defenders could see a solitary parachute drifting down before the plane disappeared.

Hastily the anti-aircraft gunners ran out to secure it to find that there was a strange metal cylinder attached to the 'chute. It was marked clearly 'not explosive'. Mystified the gunners carried it back to the HQ of one of the senior German commanders, Graf von Schmettow.

For a while they examined the device gingerly until they found that the Graf's name was wrapped in an oiled envelope attached to it. They opened the envelope and in it found a request from 'Eisenhower's HQ'. It was for the Germans to reconnect the severed cable link between the islands and France so that they could talk over the phone to a 'senior member of Eisenhower's staff'.

Under the circumstances von Schmettow had to refuse; he was afraid of Huffmeier and the local Gestapo. Indeed von Schmettow, knowing that the British had agents on the island, published a message intended for Minister of Propaganda Goebbels in the local paper. It read: 'The three Island Fortresses will faithfully hold out to the last. With this we salute our Führer and our Fatherland!'

That seemed to be the end of the affair and its connection with 'Operation Grab'. But for Admiral Huffmeier it was only the beginning. The naval fire-eater must have told himself that the Amis wanted to talk the German occupiers into surrendering. Why? Because they presented a problem to the Allied rear. Naturally his main concern was to carry the fight to the Continent. But if at the moment that was not feasible he'd try to find out more about the Americans over the Channel and transmit the information to Berlin.

By now Huffmeier knew that in the German capital, the old German secret service, the Abwehr, under Rear-Admiral Canaris, had been forcibly incorporated into the SD, the SS's own secret service, led by that cunning ex-lawyer General Schellenberg. The SS, bolder, still confident of final victory and more aggressive than the gentlemen of the old Abwehr, would be grateful for any information. Now that the German Army was fleeing back to the borders of the Reich, the SS would need all the information about the Allied armies they could get. In particular, now that he had just learned from the strange cylinder, the location of Allied HQ in France would be very useful for a German bombing attack, or even some kind of clandestine operation.

Unknown to Huffmeier, the Abwehr had already tried to find out the exact location of Eisenhower's tactical headquarters prior to D-Day. A Frenchwoman of Russian descent, Natalie Serguiew, had been told by her German handler to apply for a visa to enter Britain as a nurse. 'Tramp' as she was code-named by the Abwehr did so successfully. Among the tasks she was given was to find out where Eisenhower's SHAEF HQ was. To what purpose is not recorded.*

'Tramp' was soon working for MI5 where she was code-named 'Treasure'. But she proved a difficult agent for her female control, Mary Sherer. She had many personal problems, including that of her dog 'Frisson'. She had been forced to leave her beloved pet behind in quarantine in Gibraltar where she had been recruited as a double agent. Her work was affected. Then 'Frisson' died and 'Tramp-Treasure' vowed revenge. As Mary Sherer reported, 'this exceptionally troublesome and temperamental agent' has 'seriously threatened that if the dog doesn't arrive soon she will not work anymore'. Now with the dog dead, Serguiew carried out her threat and she went even further. She took up with her German control once more, then got cold feet and told Mary Sherer what she had done. That finished her with British Intelligence. Someone else took over her transmission to her Abwehr masters, while she was passed on to General de Gaulle's Free French Intelligence in London. The transfer was indicative of what the British spymasters thought of the French service. So 'Tramp-Treasure' passed out of the secret history of WWII and the Germans did not learn the true location of Eisenhower's HQ until it was too late.

Now it was, in a way, up to the 'Madman of the Islands', Huffmeier. The Nazi admiral knew a lot about staff officers and their bosses. He had fretted as one for several months on the damaged *Scharnhorst* when he would dearly have longed to go back to sea in a fighting command. Staff officers, Huffmeier knew, liked the comfort and security of a headquarters as far as possible from the front line. From the strange capsule addressed

*When the author asked Skorzeny why he hadn't attempted a commando raid on Britain prior to D-Day to find out Allied dispositions, etc. he replied it had been considered, but rejected, because Britain was 'too well buttoned up'.

to Count von Schmettow he knew, too, that Eisenhower's HQ had to be in France. Why else restore the telephone cable so that von Schmettow could arrange the surrender of the islands at the highest level? Besides, hadn't the plane which had dropped the capsule flown off in the direction of the Continent? So putting two and two together, it was reasonable to suppose that, if the Americans were already in the German frontier, the Ami commander's HQ might well be a couple of hundred kilometres to the rear, perhaps even in Normandy just across the water from the islands.

Despite von Schmettow's reaction to the first American attempt to make him surrender, they tried again. On the afternoon of Friday 22 September, an American patrol boat *FK 56*, commanded by 1st Lt Meyer, approached Guernsey under a white flag. The Germans watched the little craft intently, but they let it reach St Pierre Port without doing anything. Then a German officer met the American boat and encountered a 'Major from Eisenhower's Headquarters', as the Germans recorded at the time.

The US Major asked the German officer if he knew the latest develop-ments on the Western Front? Did the German know that all of northern France had been liberated and that Allied forces had passed through Belgium and Luxembourg and were now actually attacking inside Germany in the Eifel region? Finished with the details of the American victories, the 'Major from Eisenhower's headquarters' asked the German whether his chief, von Schmettow, was prepared to surrender.

Back at St Pierre's Port von Schmettow was not prepared to do so. He told the German officer to go back to the 'Major' and tell him he was fully aware of the situation on the mainland (he wasn't of course, but he was putting a brave face on the whole business). He wasn't prepared to discuss the American offer any further.

Presumably feeling that he had been well and truly put in his place, the 'Major from Eisenhower's Headquarters' set off again for his base. Unfortunately the whole garrison of the Channel Islands hadn't been informed that the US craft was flying the white flag of truce. At all events it was a grey, overcast September day and *FK 56*'s white flag had been become wound round the flag post by the wind. The result was that the German gun batteries on Alderney opened fire on the American boat. The huge guns missed and the shaken Americans ploughed through the choppy waters safely and on to their base. But not before the craft had been observed by no less a person than Admiral Huffmeier.

He observed *FK 56* closely as she escaped from the Alderney area and set course for Le Cateret on the French mainland. Huffmeier, like most German navy men who had served in the West, knew this part of the coast intimately. St Nazaire, Lorient, etc. had been used by the Kriegsmarine as safe havens ever since the Germans had conquered France.

Now he concluded that *FK 56*, carrying the 'Major from Eisenhower's Headquarters', was heading for either Cherbourg or Cateret, and that the American Supreme Commander's HQ had been established somewhere in that general area.

In the event Admiral Huffmeier was wrong, but he wasn't far wrong. Eisenhower's headquarters was located at the little Norman port of Granville, where that day Eisenhower was being ordered to take more bed-rest by his chief surgeon, Albert Kenner, due to the fact that he had injured his old West Point 'football knee' once again.

Code-named 'Shellburst', Eisenhower's advanced headquarters was described by Kay Summersby, Eisenhower's driver and lover, thus:

> In early September, our advanced headquarters was in Granville, a fishing port, where Ike had a house with a picture postcard view of Mont St Michel, the ancient Benedictine Abbey that, when the tide was high, rose like a magic island in the bay.

Ironically enough 'Ike' was housed in a villa which bore the same name of that of his bête-noir to come – Villa Montgomery.

Even more ironic was the fact that Granville, a mere score or so miles from the Channel Islands, was the site of a daring raid by Admiral Huffmeier's men six months later in March '45. Then the men of 'Division Kanada' would catch the US garrison completely by surprise. They would take some sixty Americans prisoners, seize two small freighters and return successfully to the island fortress to be awarded the Iron Cross and more importantly, a spoonful of precious jam each!

The mind boggles at the thought that if Huffmeier had known that back in September 1944, when he still had 30,000 men under command, unfit as most of them were, he might well have captured or killed the Supreme Commander and perhaps changed the whole course of the war in the West.

But on that 23 September 1944, when he made his report to Berlin that he suspected Eisenhower's HQ was somewhere in Normandy, he didn't know. So the firebrand was fated to disappear into a POW camp together with the rest of the Channel Islands' 'Division Kanada', his chance to make history failed and forgotten.

A month before Huffmeier sent off his signal stating that he believed Eisenhower, or at least his headquarters, was now in France, the Supreme Commander met 'Joan of Arc' in the French capital for the first time. 'That damned new Joan of Arc,' as President Roosevelt called the detested General de Gaulle, commander of the Free French, had arrived in France illegally, as far as the Americans were concerned, that summer.

They had not wanted him in the war zone; they preferred he should be kept out of the way in North Africa. Indeed Roosevelt had given strict instructions that the Free French general should not be allowed to leave Algiers and start meddling in the affairs of a France soon to be liberated. De Gaulle thought differently. He had dodged the Americans and had flown to Normandy, landing with only a few litres of fuel left in the plane's engines.

Now as he met General Eisenhower in the newly liberated French capital, where he had been sniped probably by renegade Frenchmen and women of the kind that Skorzeny had left behind as 'sleepers', he was full of his usual gripes that always annoyed the Anglo-Americans. As de Gaulle himself wrote after the war:

> We congratulated each other on the happy outcome of events in Paris. I did not hide from him, however, how dissatisfied I was with Gerow's* attitude as I was entering my own capital and grasping the cauldron in my hands.

Naturally Eisenhower, used to dealing with touchy foreign allies, 'a bunch of goddam prima donnas', as he called them privately, smoothed over the difficulties and then confided in the tall, beaky-nosed de Gaulle a secret. As de Gaulle described the exchange: 'Eisenhower said he was going to install his headquarters in Versailles.' For once de Gaulle didn't complain. He knew that if he had trouble with the very strong French Communist Party, which had played a major part in the Resistance and expected a reward for their efforts, the Americans would step in and help him. Trouble near the Allied – read, American – Supreme Headquarters would simply not be allowed.

Naturally Eisenhower would move his HQ to Versailles just outside the French capital, not only for military reasons, but also for political ones. His masters in London and Washington, in particular President Roosevelt, wanted to keep a tight rein on the French maverick. Versailles would suit their purpose perfectly. Apparently de Gaulle didn't mind. He wrote: 'I approved the move believing it a good idea to have the Allied Commander-in-Chief lodged outside Paris . . . It would be useful that he should be near.'

That August Eisenhower (perhaps for political reasons) had revealed to the French prima donna a secret the Germans would have given their eye teeth to have known in September 1944. But as summer gave way to autumn 1944, the Germans were already beginning to find out that

---

*General Gerow, commander of the US V Corps, who incidentally was married to a French wife, and whose relatives were later accused of having collaborated with the Germans. One wonders if de Gaulle didn't have a hand in that accusation which almost ruined Gerow's career.

Eisenhower had moved his headquarters from Bushy Park, England to France and Versailles. De Gaulle was not particularly security conscious and he had on his staff officers, whom the British SIS thought untrustworthy and inclined to betray secrets for political or monetary reasons. As Group Captain Freddie Winterbotham, guardian of the ULTRA secret and head of Air Intelligence once remarked:*

> We in the 'Old Firm' [Secret Service] never trusted de Gaulle and his Free French in London during the war or Prince Bernhard of the Netherlands for that matter. They were always nosing about our offices. And if anyone was going to blab a secret to the enemy it would have been those two or their minions.

Eisenhower knew of course that it was important to keep the location of his main headquarters as secret as possible for as long as possible. His naval aide and PR man, Lt Commander Butcher, noted in his diary for 9 September 1944:

> Ike has ordered operational secrecy for Allied forces pushing towards Germany . . . We are going so rapidly that if he [Eisenhower] permits prompt dissemination of news, the hard-pressed Germans, with their communication disrupted, can keep their war maps up to date by listening to the BBC.

Naturally 'Ike' would still continue to be photographed, visiting his troops, conferring with other Allied generals, etc. That was important as a morale factor. But as all troop movements would be censored so that the Germans could not use this information for their own purposes, so would the details of where exactly he went on his infrequent visits to his soldiers. But as the German front started to bog down later that same September and the enemy began to capture higher ranking officers, who knew the location of Supreme Headquarters, we can assume that by the time Skorzeny started his planning for 'Operation Grab', he had a fair idea where the Supreme Commander might be.

It would be surprising if he didn't by then, for three very high-ranking Americans were captured by the Germans in early November. They not only knew the ULTRA secret but were also members of the OSS, and had extensive knowledge of the Supreme Command and both the American and British Intelligence systems.

It had all started as a weekend joyride when Gertrude Legendre, an American society woman and noted big game hunter, decided to take a short leave from her position as head of the OSS message centre in Paris.

*To the author.

She left for Nancy, Patton's HQ, where an old friend, Major Maxwell J Papurt, also of the OSS and naturally as such into the secret of the location of Supreme Headquarters, borrowed a jeep for an outing to the front. With them they took a third OSS officer, Lt Commander Robert Jennings, stationed in Paris at Supreme HQ itself.

From Nancy they drove to Luxembourg and from there they took the country road to the former German frontier, marked by the Sauer river. Here, ever since the Americans had been thrown back in September after their first attempt to drive into the Reich, the front had been quiet and lightly held. Probably confused by the lack of activity, the three in their jeep ran the length of the Sauer for some five miles until they reached Wallendorf, which straddled the border river. Then they made a bad mistake. They somehow crossed to the German side and were promptly captured by the understandably jubilant Germans. Not only had they captured two senior US officers, they had also taken a woman prisoner, the first American woman to be captured by the Germans during the campaign in North-West Europe. Back at OSS HQ, they were less than pleased at this German 'first'. As the OSS report on their capture recorded: '[they] are in a position to give away extremely damaging information.'

They were. At first the Germans at the local corps headquarters in Trier were slow to realise that their prisoners were of great importance and members of the OSS. But when their interrogation started in earnest the German Intelligence officers soon discovered that the three prisoners knew something of SHAEF's Special Counter-Intelligence (SCI). This organisation operated on the basis of the ULTRA decodes and double agents who worked both for the Allies and the Germans themselves. More importantly for Skorzeny, the three of them identified the location of the various secret intelligence agencies working for Eisenhower's head-quarters in Versailles and other parts of the French capital.

Although Papurt tried to mislead his interrogators, documents found on his person revealed the names and functions of a total of thirty key SCI agents and their locations not only in Versailles-Paris but throughout Allied-held Europe. That November he was taken away immediately to a special prison camp at Diez near Limburg on the Rhine, where on 29 November he was to undergo an intensive interrogation by Schellenberg's SD. Whether by accident or design, he was killed by an Allied bombing raid before that took place. Papurt was the second person with the knowledge about ULTRA who after being captured by the Germans died in captivity, the other being P C Cadia.

The originator of that unfortunate joyride, which resulted in the death of Major Papurt, Mrs Legendre, was allowed to live. Perhaps the Germans thought she was the major's mistress or something of that kind. Using her strong personality and cunning she managed to escape detection. Then after six months in prison she leaped from a prison train during a switching operation near the Swiss frontier and escaped to Dulles' OSS HQ in Berne. Immediately she was flown back to Washington in deep secrecy and thereafter, probably in disgrace for her wilful disobedience of orders, which might have uncovered the greatest intelligence coup of all times, ULTRA, she disappeared from the secret intelligence scene.

So now due to the ill discipline of the OSS operatives and other leaks and sources, Skorzeny knew a great deal about Eisenhower's Versailles HQ; and what an HQ it was. The actual numbers of men and women of half a dozen nationalities were kept secret for obvious military reasons during the war and after it, for probably more personal ones. With the dire shortage of men at the front, it would have been difficult to explain away the huge staff at Versailles, the office workers, planners, servants and the usual flunkeys and visiting 'firemen'.

Some authorities maintain that 21,000 soldiers worked at Supreme HQ, the equivalent of a division and a half of infantry. Each of Eisenhower's key staff, some twenty-seven of them, did have large personal staffs, however. For example Scottish General Kenneth Strong had a staff of 1,000.

Visiting Strong, known behind his back at the 'Hangman's dilemma' on account of the fact that his chin was so sloping it would be difficult to keep a hangman's noose in place, one of his former London staff Noel Annan noticed the change since that time in his former boss. 'By now Strong had the sleek, well-fed look of a senior staff officer, who had adopted the lifestyle of the top American brass.'

Annan learned too as he started working at Versailles himself that winter of 1944:

> It was not as if the vast staff helped Eisenhower to take strategic decisions; they had already been taken at meetings between Eisenhower, his army group commanders and General Patton ... As a result the plans SHAEF made were a series of compromises and the staff spent more of their time producing papers to justify these decisions to the Combined Chiefs of Staff than in producing the data on which plans could be made.

As Annan and others saw it from outside and inside, most of the soldiers employed at the vast headquarters, well away from the blood, the cold and the misery of the front in Germany, had found a well-upholstered sinecure, obeying the official line that the German army was beaten. Strong was to say later, after disaster had struck, that intelligence officers were regarded as defeatist if they didn't believe the end of the war was in sight. As Annan commented, 'all the warlords [he meant the Versailles big shots], despite their rivalries, agreed that this was so'. As the peacetime recruiting sergeants might have phrased it, at Versailles the

Above left: **1.** Hitler at his home 'on the mountain' in Bavaria, 1939.

Above right: **2.** Georg Elser, the humble German carpenter and would-be assassin. Here in Gestapo arrest, after torture by 'Gestapo' Mueller, showing Himmler how he planted the bomb with which he had intended to kill the dictator in Munich.

Right: **3.** Gestapo Mueller who tortured a confession out of Elser and made Best and Stevens confess.

Above: **4.** The Burgerbrau-Keller, Munich, 8 November 1939 after Elser's failed assassination attempt on Hitler.

Left: **5.** Reichsführer SS Himmler, planner of the kidnapping of Stevens and Best, the two SIS agents allegedly behind the plot to kill the Führer. Later he would be the victim of an alleged British assassination attempt.

Above: **6.** 'The intellectual thug', as Shirer called him: Alfred Naujocks of the *SD* who carried out the Venlo kidnapping of the two British SIS agents.

Right: **7.** 'The Man with the Iron Heart', Hitler called him. Reinhard Heydrich, assassinated in the spring of 1942 by Czech patriots flown in from Britain. At whose order, Czech or British, is still unclear to this day.

8. The author with Heydrich's widow on the island of Fehmarn. She holds a christening plate given to her on the birth of their son by the head of the SA, Captain Ernst Roehm, murdered by Heydrich's men on Hitler's orders in 1934.

9. Heydrich's Mercedes wrecked by the assassins' grenade on the outskirts of Prague, 1942. Some experts maintained that the grenade which finally killed him was impregnated with spores of anthrax.

Right: **10.** Heydrich was so notorious that the 'Hangman of Prague' was featured on the front cover of *Time* magazine. Hollywood made a movie of his career, the only German save Rommel to be featured in WWII in a 'Tinseltown' film.

Below: **11.** The site of the wartime Paris *Sphinx* brothel, once partly owned by Goering and one of the alleged rallying points for Skorzeny's assassins.

12. Eisenhower's SHAEF HQ as it is today.

13. Eisenhower's villa in Paris.

Above left: **14.** Obersturmbannführer Peiper, who led the 6th Panzer Army's point. Skorzeny was to go in with him.

Above right: **15.** Peiper receiving final instructions.

16. American survivors of the VIII Corps front, through which Skorzeny and his assassins hoped to drive.

17. The Peiper-Skorzeny infiltration commenced here – just over the German border at Losheim, Belgium.

18. Here, for Skorzeny, it ended when he was severely wounded in the eye at the famed Hôtel du Moulin, Ligneuville, Belgium.

Nazi Who Saved Duce Boasts Of Plot to Slay Eisenhower

By Ed Lawrence
Stars and Stripes Staff Writer

WITH THIRD INF. DIV., May 18.—Lt. Col. Otto R. Skorzeny, scar-faced, 6 foot 4 professional Nazi kidnaper and killer, today boasted to his Third Div. captors of having master-minded a plot to slay Gen. Eisenhower last winter and of having engineered the escape of Benito Mussolini in September, 1943.

Skorzeny bragged that he and his picked killers kept the entire Western Front in a state of alert for several months because of the plot.

Disguised in GI uniforms, Skorzeny's men tried to infiltrate American lines early in the Ardennes offensive under pretense of bringing German prisoners to SHAEF for questioning. They hoped to get close enough to Gen. Eisenhower to kill him, but American troops foiled the plot by capturing some of the assassins.

The Waffen SS giant smiled as he recounted how he and 81 Nazi paratroopers had swooped in gliders to a mountain hotel at Frensasso to free Mussolini. In spite of 250 armed Italian guards, they spirited the one-time Fascist chief away without a shot being fired, Skorzeny said.

Skorzeny explained that Hitler took the capture of Mussolini as a personal blow. So Himmler summoned Skorzeny from his Eastern Front post and instructed him to rescue the former dictator.

Skorzeny, chief of the sabotage division of the Nazi counter-intelligence service, assembled a task force and they boarded gliders at Rome. They were joined by a German cub plane. A second SS detachment left Rome by automobile.

Crashing his glider on a steep grade Skorzeny and eight others rushed the hotel where Il Duce was a prisoner. The other gliders landed and within 15 minutes Mussolini was in the German cub, headed for Vienna.

19. The first post-war press reports on the Ike murder plan. From *Stars and Stripes*, 19 May 1945.

20. Close to the Napoleon Cross, the crossroads at Poteau, Belgium, the rallying point for the Skorzeny assassination teams.

21. The bridge at Aywaille, Belgium, five miles from the Meuse river where the first jeep team was captured and confessed to the Eisenhower assassination plan.

CRIMES BRANCH - SUMMARY WORK.

SPJGI #_____   OTHER #_____   DATE OF SUMMARY 11 Jul 45

IMMEDIATE SOURCE: Ltr W. S. Branch, Hq 12th Army Group dated 28 June 45

PLACE OF OFFENSE: Malmedy, Liege, Stavelot, Belgium   DATE: 16 Dec-25 Jan

OFFENSES: Wearing U.S. uniforms obtained from Red Cross packages.
          Plan for the assassination of Gen. EISENHOWER

ORGANIZATION OF ACCUSED: 150 Panzer Brigade   SKORZENNE BAND

NAMES OF ACCUSED	Nationality	Rank	Serial #	Present Status or Locat'n
HESSE,	German	Oberfeldwebel		POW
SKORZENE,	German	Unknown	Unknown	Unknown
n. SCHULTZ, Guenther Jos.		Lt		PW
MEISSNER		Hauptmann & Dienststellenleiter		
SKORZENY		ss Sturmbannfuehrer		
WEISS		Hauptmann & Dienstellenleiter		
ALBERT		Oberleutnant		
BLAU		Leutnant		

(see over)

INTENDED

NAMES OF VICTIMS	Nationality	Rank	Serial #	Present Status or Locat'n
EISENHOWER, Dwight	American	5*Gen		

NAMES OF WITNESSES	Nationality	Rank	Serial #	Present Status or Locat'n
STASCHKO, Fritz	German	Unteroff-izier	PWSN 31C 792 757	ROMILLY, France
ECKE, Klaus) also	German	PW's		(Organ: 3rd Co.Fusileer Rg
BUSCHOF,) at ROMILLY, France				27, Volksgrenidier Div 12

DESCRIPTIVE SUMMARY OF OFFENSES: Members of 150 Panzer Brigade wore America
uniforms from Red Cross packages from 16 Dec 1944-25 Jan 1945 at
MALMEDY, LIEGE, & STAVELOT, Belgium. They were to sabotage communications, attack headquarters & possibly kill Gen. EISENHOWER. Plan
called for infiltration thru American lines to Gen. EISENHOWER's headquarters and was to be executed following the Von Rundstedt push in
January 45. Because the push was repulsed, the plan was deferred.

22. US Army trial document including Skorzeny in Dachau. This was soon
changed on orders from above (from whom?).

23. Close to the Meuse river where men of the 8th Armoured Brigade blew up the second killer jeep team.

Above left: **24.** Il Duce, Mussolini on the left. He met his end at the hands of his 'new Romans' in the last month of the war.

Above right: **25.** Prime Minster Churchill, a target of Germans, Iraqis and Greeks at various times during the war. He survived even the December 1944 attempt in Athens, when his former allies, the Greek partisans, tried to blow him up.

Left: **26.** Wing-Commander Basil Templeman-Rooke who led the RAF bombing raid on the Eagle's Nest on 25 April 1945 in an attempt to kill Hitler.

Below: **27.** Monty's back-up team in the Ardennes. Men of the 51st Highland Division's Black Watch marching to the Meuse stop-line. Later men of the same regiment would capture Heinrich Himmler, who was allegedly assassinated on Churchill's orders.

28. Hitler's original home before the bombing by the RAF.

29. The Eagle's Nest, Berchtesgaden.

30. Hitler's mountain retreat above Berchtesgaden after the last RAF attack. But the Führer wasn't at home. Instead he died by his own hand underground in a surrounded Berlin. Today, this is the site of a luxury hotel.

31. French and American troops cheer their capture of the Eagle's Nest, 3 May 1945.

27 May, 1945.

My dear Top

Further to the good news of the death of Little H,
I feel it is imperative that we maintain a complete news blackout on the exact circumstances of this most evil man's demise.
I am sure that if it were to become public knowledge that we
had a hand in this man's demise, it would have devastating
repercussions for this country's standing. I am also sure that
this incident would complicate our relationship with our American
bretheren; under no circumstances must they discover that we
eradicated 'Little H', particularly so since we know they were so
keen to interrogate him themselves.

I am of the opinion that the special S.O.E./P.W.E.
Committee and team can now be dissolved, even though Mallet is
still negotiating with W.S. in Sweden. Perhaps you could let me
know your opinion on this matter.

Brendan Bracken

The Rt.Hon. the Earl of Selborne,
    Ministry of Economic Warfare,
        Berkeley Square House,
            Berkeley Square,
                W.1.

32. A faked letter concerning Heinrich Himmler's death. It is now alleged that
Himmler was murdered, with Churchill's knowledge and agreement.

great majority of the staff had found 'a home away from home . . . a cushy number'.

Eisenhower, the obscure colonel of four years before looking forward to a slippered retirement on a poor pension, harassed all the time by his shrewish wife Mamie, certainly had. Soon he'd be a four-star general, a hitherto unthinkable promotion for him. Now he had an 18th-century French villa as a home away from home. He wore silk underwear and had black servants – 'darkies', he called them. Impotent as he was, he had a former model as a mistress, and an intimate coterie of friends, cronies and hangers-on, who shielded him from the hard realities of the winter front, which he rarely visited anyway.

There was his chief-of-staff, General Bedell 'Red' Smith, and his mistress. Red's temper was as fierce as the colour of his hair. He customarily referred to the female WAC soldiers at the HQ as 'GIs with built-in foxholes'. General Everell Hughes was another. He was Ike's 'eyes and ears', crony and card-playing buddy (also with mistress in tow) who provided the Supreme Commander with all the latest tittle-tattle about his fellow officers.

Then came 'Tex', his booming-voice aide; Telek, the poodle dog; 'Mickey', his 'striker'* who wrote letters home to Mamie for him, all commanded in a way by Navy Lt Commander Butcher, his PR man and former radio executive. 'Butch' also supervised the running of his home centred on Marie Antoinette's Petit Trianon, the splendid 18th-century baroque structure which had been part of the little estate she had created before she was so cruelly executed, in order to play 'simple' milkmaid, dressed naturally in fabulously expensive 'simple' silken gowns. One wonders if Eisenhower ever remembered the statement attributed to the ill-fated Queen when told the peasants were without bread, 'then give them cake', and that in the end one had to pay the penalty for a life divorced from reality, in Ike's case, the fighting front.

Up to a couple of months before, the house which Eisenhower's staff had picked for him after his move from Granville had been the home of no less a person than Field Marshal Gerd von Rundstedt, the Supreme Commander's opponent in Normandy and soon to be his opponent again in the Battle of the Bulge. Here the aged German Field Marshal, with the terrible wrinkled face, had indulged himself in fine French wines and good cognac and had, as he was wont to remark, 'enjoyed the war because the peace was going to be terrible.'

There at the villa in Germaine-en-Laye, he had enjoyed a kind of tranquil existence when off-duty. But the very isolation of the villa made it a security officer's nightmare. This was increased by the fact that the security men were well aware that the Germans knew every nook and

*Batman.

85

cranny of the 18th-century house. After all the 'Krauts' had occupied the place for four years and had indeed made certain additions to it, such as air-raid shelters (never used), which would make an ideal hiding place for any would-be assassins.

That winter before the storm broke, General Eisenhower had become a security risk . . . But the American officer, who faced that security man's 'nightmare' daily was the 'low man on the totem pole', Lt Colonel Gordon Sheen of the US Corps of Counter-Intelligence, who reported directly to General Strong, though neither Strong nor anyone else for that matter seemed particularly interested in his reports. For not only was Sheen a mere 'half colonel' in a headquarters where such lowly creatures were, as Strong's American colleagues phrased it 'a dime a dozen', he was an officer of a military unit which officially had ceased to exist in the continental United States – and that at the express order of President Roosevelt himself.

CHAPTER II

Even Staff Officers Wet Their Knickers

After 1921, when as his own son James stated, Franklin D Roosevelt became the 'father with the dead legs' due to the polio which had attacked that year, FDR started to hide his true feelings from everyone. As someone wrote of the afflicted President, he was accustomed 'to play his cards so close to his chest that the ink rubbed off on his shirt'.

Now the future President, who was in constant pain and had to hide his true condition from everyone but his intimates, deemed to show little interest in his cousin and wife, Eleanor. She had already turned away from him on account of an affair he had had before he became a victim of the crippling affliction. Now she frequented the company of notorious Washington lesbians, whom FDR called half-jokingly 'she-males'.

But by the time President Roosevelt was into his third term, allegations were made that Eleanor, who pretty much ran her own life separate from the President, was apparently having an affair with a man – and a communist sympathiser to boot!

The allegations came from an obscure part of the US Army, the Corps of Counter-Intelligence (CIC). It had been founded on New Year's Day, 1942 when the old Corps of Intelligence Police had been re-named. Both the old and new organisations were virtually unknown within Army circles and would remain so.

Now, however, this obscure counter-intelligence organisation came to the attention of the President himself and FDR didn't like one bit what he was hearing from it. Apparently the CIC had bugged the room occupied by S/Sgt Joseph Lash of the US Army Air Corps. The noncom was a friend of both Roosevelt and Eleanor, and in the case of the President's wife he seemed to be more than just friendly. According to the CIC report submitted to the President, a 'sexual encounter' had taken place between the low-ranking noncom and Mrs Roosevelt in the hotel room that the counter-intelligent agents had bugged.

According to those around the President at the time, FDR flew into a towering rage. He ordered that Lash be shipped overseas within the next ten hours. Now the President turned his attention on this new intelligence agency and demanded it should cease its activities in the USA. Thus it was that the CIC wound up its operations stateside and those of its senior agents who managed to survive the 'Washington Bloodbath' were undoubtedly glad to be posted overseas as swiftly as possible. For they guessed there wouldn't be much promotion in the future for those who had once worked for the now disgraced counter-intelligence unit.

Lt Colonel Gordon Sheen was one of the fortunate few who survived by securing a swift posting to the UK and thence to North Africa. Finally he was appointed to Supreme Headquarters, where he had become the most senior officer in the CIC and probably in Europe too. Not that that counted for much. Sheen and his subordinates were shadowy figures, fighting to survive among a multitude of intelligence agencies, dominated by the OSS. Nor were the CIC men particularly liked by their fellow soldiers, who regarded them as a kind of 'boss's nark', reporting on them for any breach of security and the like.

Of course, Sheen must have thought he had hit the jackpot when he was appointed to the Supreme Headquarters and the Parisian fleshpots which went with that appointment. Here he had to report to General Strong. But Strong with a thousand staff under his command was not particularly interested in counter-intelligence (at least not yet). He left the rounding up of spies, informers, sleeper agents, etc. to lesser mortals.

Naturally Sheen, who seems to have been a busybody and a nervous type for an ex-policeman, knew he had to justify his position at Supreme HQ. He realised, of course, that his first priority was the HQ itself, located in the Trianon Palace, It was a jewel in the French crown, a national treasure, where in 1919 the Treaty of Versailles had been signed. Even the Allies had to be careful in such premises. So it was that only a limited number of the highest-ranking officers were accommodated there: the G-1, G-2, G-3 and G-4, plus a few of Eisenhower's own special staff. Any German agent knocking out the Trianon and those key staff officers who worked in it would naturally deliver a severe body blow to the Allied war effort on the Continent.

The CIC also knew that there were plenty of German agents and sleepers at large in France – Sheen was receiving reports of them being captured virtually every day. If these agents were fanatical enough or adequately bribed, they might well carry out any plan the Germans devised, however daring. Indeed ever since the D-Day landings there had been examples of French agents in German employ attacking British and US troops. Even as the troops had left the beaches they had been sniped at by renegade Frenchmen – and Frenchwomen, too. Trucks of the vital supply unit, the 'Red Ball Express', had also been attacked by what the Americans called 'bush-whackers'. By early September Sheen's agents in the field were reporting that not only were they picking up sleeper agents all along the frontier with Germany (and in Paris, too), but they were also capturing new agents being dropped by parachute straight from Germany itself.

Agent Ib Melchior, son of the famous Danish opera singer, now attached to the US XII Corps on the German-Luxembourg-Saar border, recalled long afterwards how he caught his first enemy parachute agent. Parachutes had been dropped in his area and Melchior and his comrades from CIC were on patrol looking for the parachutists when they were stopped by a mud-stained little Frenchman who started to cry with joy when he saw the Americans' jeep.

He explained that he had been a slave worker in Germany for two years, but had escaped and for two days and nights 'he'd run, crept and stumbled towards his beloved France and the American liberators'. The Frenchman seemed genuine enough, but Melchior had his doubts. He decided to check the man's body for the tell-tale red marks of parachute harness. Nothing. The Frenchman seemed clear.

Melchior was about to let him go on his way when he noticed that the man was wearing low-cut shoes, now muddy and scuffed. They certainly weren't the boots a parachutist would wear. 'Take off your shoes and socks,' he ordered the Frenchman. Slowly and reluctantly the man obeyed. Melchior took one look and snapped angrily, 'What specific acts of sabotage were you to carry out?' The man's feet had been the give-away.

> On each dirty foot and ankle were the clean outlines of double-wrapped, recently discarded bandage, just the kind of bandage a parachutist might use to support his feet when jumping, wearing low-cut shoes instead of the giveaway boots, to avoid twisting an ankle in a night drop.

Melchior's capture of the French saboteur was typical of the kind of reports that Sheen was receiving from both General Bradley's 12th Army Group and General Devers' Sixth, both groups in position along the frontier with Germany from the Swiss border right up to Holland. A half company of the 15th Engineers doing road work had been attacked by seventy Germans in US uniform yelling 'GI', for some reason or other. Recently captured front-line German prisoners had express orders that any captured Ami equipment or uniform should be sent immediately to Osnabruck in northern Germany. Why Osnabruck, so far from the front, Sheen pondered. Then Sheen, a man of little or no importance in the great sprawling Supreme Headquarters, had his breakthrough: one that now brought him to the attention of his superiors, in particular, Eisenhower's Chief-of-Intelligence, General Strong.

On 26 October 1944, at precisely one o'clock in the afternoon, the signal centre of Army Group B, commanded by Field Marshal Model, the army which would fight the coming Battle of the Bulge, received a teleprinter message from Führer HQ. It read: 'The Führer has ordered the formation of a special unit of approximately two battalions for use on the Western Front in special operations and reconnaissance . . .'

The order was crystal clear. It asked for volunteers from all three services, army, navy and air force. They had to be top-fit, expert in hand-to-hand combat, and have a knowledge of English. If possible they should know 'the American dialect'. 'This order will forthwith be made known to all units and services.' There was no doubt that it would. For the order was signed by no less a person that Field Marshal Keitel.

General Westphal, the Army Group's chief-of-staff, immediately distributed the strange order to all units, other than the garrisons of the Channel Islands, the besieged fortresses on the Atlantic coast, Lorient, St Nazaire, La Rochelle and Royan, still held by the Germans, and non-German units in the Wehrmacht. Obviously security was important, save for one thing: details of where the volunteers were to be sent.

They were to be dispatched by 10 November to '*Dienststelle Skorzeny*' at Friedenthal near Oranienburg concentration camp. Here Reichsführer SS Himmler, who seemingly was in charge of the recruits, would report their number to Keitel. But before that report could be made to the wooden-headed Field Marshal, the order was known to the Allies, including chief of security, Sheen, who, like the men who decoded the Keitel signal, must have been absolutely flabbergasted at it.

It didn't take a crystal ball for Sheen and others in Intelligence to realise that something was afoot. Two battalions of English-speaking troops were to be employed in reconnaissance. That meant a long-range mission behind Allied lines. Add to that the Keitel order requesting volunteers who could speak the 'American dialect' and Sheen could only conclude that whatever this long-range mission was, it was going to be carried out against US troops.

But why this new formation, which would report to Skorzeny at his headquarters in Friedenthal? From what Sheen already knew about the French renegades, sleeper agents and parachutist, there seemed to be enough of them already operating behind Allied lines. What could the man, who had rescued Mussolini the previous year and had since carried out similar top-level covert missions, want with two new battalions?

Sheen must have concluded even then before the great flap commenced that Germany's leading commando, the scarfaced giant, was after some Allied 'big fish'. But who? We don't know whether Sheen communicated his suspicions to General Strong as November gave way to December. From all accounts of events at that time, there seems to have been no noticeable tightening of security at Allied Headquarters in Versailles, despite the uneasy feeling, vague at present, among Intelligence circles that all was not well at the front. Indeed two British officers, Captain Pryce-Jones, once on Strong's staff in London, and Wing Commander Jim

Rose, head of the Air Section in Hut Three at Bletchley Park, had warned Ike's chief-of-intelligence that something was up after Strong had maintained Germany might well lose the war by Christmas. The debonair Pryce-Jones had sat on the edge of Strong's desk, swinging his leg, and had snorted, 'If you believe that you'll believe anything.'

But if some doubted that the 'boys will be home for Christmas', as some pundits both in the States and at Supreme Headquarters predicted, and Sheen worried that there was something big and dangerous in the offing, the CIC man apparently did little about it. Perhaps lowly lieutenant-colonel that he was, he felt it better to wait and gather more information before he'd implement more intensive measures to protect the big brass.

So life at the great headquarters proceeded in its customary manner. There were conferences and there were parties. Lovers quarrelled and clerks made love behind the filing cabinets. Petty rivalries developed between competing staff officers. Talk was of the rising prices in the capital's black market restaurants and how the GIs from the front were ruining the reputation of the US Army with their antics on pass in Paris's 'pig alley' (Place Pigalle). The Parisians maintained that the Germans had been much better behaved. In the American officers' opinion the 'white mice', or US military police, were too lenient with these drunken louts from the front. Paris should be placed off limits to them as had been done in Naples. And virtually everyone still believed in what Major Annan of Strong's staff called the 'Happy Hypothesis'. This suggested that the German army had been so shattered in Normandy and battered in Russia that it was only a matter of two or three months before the war would end. As a worldly wise and cynical Noel Annan summed it all up, '[It was] all balls and rackets' and he wasn't referring to the game of tennis.

Skorzeny was shocked beyond measure by the Keitel circular. As he recorded later: 'I thought our operation was betrayed before it commenced. I dictated a flaming protest to the Führer's headquarters and telephoned through my decision to cancel the mission.' But Skorzeny's protest was blocked by Jodl and others. He was told to go through channels and the channels consisted of Hitler's new brother-in-law, SS General Fegelein, a vain womanising ex-SS divisional commander who was shot on Hitler's order at the end of the war as a suspected British spy and deserter.

Fegelein answered by return that the Keitel circular was very un-fortunate. 'But I had to abide by the original plan.' He, Skorzeny, had to take his chance like everyone else connected with the great counter-attack. With that the commando leader had to be satisfied! 'With a heavy heart', as he recalled, feeling that he was sending his young volunteers on a suicide mission, he continued with his preparations for 'Day X'.

His men were, for the most part, in great heart. Most of them had volunteered from desk jobs, though they were all combat-experienced, and were looking for adventure. Two thousand men had reported for 'Operation Grab', but if they were experienced soldiers and sailors, their English in many cases was limited to school standard. In the end only 200 of them were found to speak fluent English. These were mostly sailors or men who had lived in the USA and, in some cases, actually had American nationality. One or two of them had even served in the US Army.

Skorzeny soldiered on, fighting desperately to get the necessary equipment for his force which had now grown to 3,500 men. Overcoats were his first priority. They turned out not to be American, but British. Six armoured cars followed. They, too, were British. They broke down constantly and in the end they were scrapped. Slowly, bit by bit, he got his American equipment together: a handful of Shermans, several White halftracks and some cars, and fifteen American jeeps, the hardest item of all to obtain. For every German unit wanted to hang on to a captured jeep. Now what the secret unit didn't have, they made up for by camouflaging German tanks with false turrets and guns so that they looked like US armoured fighting vehicles – at least from a distance.

In particular Skorzeny was intent on obtaining the right equipment and clothing for the so-called 'Stielau Company', named after Captain Stielau, the sixth and last of the unit's commanders who had followed each other in rapid succession between 10 November and 16 December indicative of just how much importance Skorzeny placed on this particular group of eighty men, most of whom spoke good English.

The 'Stielau' Group was divided into the so-called reconnaissance group in six jeeps, each one holding three to four men, and the sabotage group in eight jeeps. If anybody was going to attempt an attack on a high-ranking Allied officer it would be these men, who were kept pretty well separate from the rest of the volunteers once they had been trained. One can understand why.

But at the beginning all of them, Stielau specialists and the ordinary rank and file of volunteers, were shipped to the major German tank training ground at Gräfenwöhr near Nuremberg. Here they were escorted into their sealed off camp by what the German soldiers called scornfully 'booty Germans', that is ethnic Germans who had volunteered for the SS. They were supposed by Skorzeny to be more trustworthy than the average German *lendser*. After all they risked being shot out of hand if they were captured for having betrayed the country of their birth.

Almost like prisoners themselves, the volunteers were sealed in by the grim-faced guards and had their paybooks taken off them immediately. With their identity thus removed, they risked being shot as deserters if they left the camp. Anyway they were forbidden to do so in the five weeks or so they spent there. As French historian Jacques Nobecourt recorded:

[one man] was actually shot for having sent home a letter giving too full a description of his existence, in contravention of the oath of full silence he had given . . . isolation was so rigorously maintained that the sick were not sent to hospital; as a precaution others were dosed against influenza and colds.

Naturally some of the volunteers were worried about being shot as spies if captured wearing Allied uniforms (that indeed would be the fate of at least twenty-eight of them after capture during the Battle of the Bulge). Even von Rundstedt worried about the legalities of that. Skorzeny soon solved the problem in his usual masterly fashion. He brought in a trained lawyer to explain to the worried soldiers that they had nothing to fear. As long as they kept their German uniforms on underneath the American ones and revealed them before opening fire, they were in the clear under 'International Law'.

Jodl was not so sanguine. In a letter, answering von Rundstedt's query about the legality of wearing a foreign uniform, he stated:

Since the Field Marshal has raised the problem we have re-examined the matter. There is no question of any infringement of international law; it is merely a war stratagem, such as the other side has used on all fronts with far more frequency than we have.

Jodl then revealed his real attitude. He went on:

Moreover, all the men selected are volunteers. They are quite aware of the possibility that they might be treated as partisans. This they have accepted; no one has forced them into it.

Furthermore there can be no question of changing the orders already given. They are as sacrosanct as all the other tactical measures laid down for the offensive.

From Jodl's letter two things are clear. One is the absolutely callousness of the German High Command towards these young volunteers who might soon be going to their deaths, not in battle, but in front of an enemy firing squad. The second is the fact that Hitler's chief-of-operations maintains that Skorzeny's operation, which on the face of it is a mere covert mission with no real tactical objective, is as important as the other major tactical operations involving whole divisions and corps numbering thousands of soldiers. Why? The answer can be only that Colonel-General Jodl knew that 'Operation Grab' involved more than just sabotage and reconnaissance.

Unaware of their probable fate and their objective, the volunteers were now put through their paces in the Gräfenwöhr Training Ground. One volunteer remembered his time in the remote camp with its sullen ethnic German SS guards thus: 'My bunk was in the block occupied by Captain Stielau's group. Almost immediately I was struck by the unusual almost unsoldierly attitude of the members of this unit.'

Soon he discovered why all the men of the special group were learning not only to improve their knowledge of the 'American dialect', but also how to act and move like GIs. The volunteer soon found out he was expected to do the same.

> In an astonishingly short time, we achieved the feeling of 'together-ness' which you usually find only at times of great stress at the front . . . At first we were mostly concerned with learning the idiom of the GIs. The showing of American films, especially war films, played a great role in our training. Then came the day we were sent to American POW camps where we mixed with GIs and gained the impression that we were developing into perfect Yankees.

It was a dangerous form of instruction. By now even the easy-going American prisoners, who in the main were not as well organised as their British fellow POWs (the US Army didn't believe in teaching its soldiers what to do when taken prisoner, save to keep their mouths shut), had become suspicious of newcomers in the camps. They had organised midnight 'kangeroo courts' to 'try' anyone they suspected of being a 'stool-pigeon' or a German infiltrator. Soldiers found guilty were usually discovered hanging at the end of a length of rope and declared suicides; or disappeared for good into the yellow noxious mess of the camp's 'thunderboxes'.

Still working against time Skorzeny knocked his force into shape. As he saw it, it was not his job to turn them into special forces troops, guerrillas or the like. They were all trained, battle-experienced soldiers anyway. What he wanted from time to time was that they change their whole pattern of behaviour.

As Skorzeny saw it, nationality was a matter of basic instincts, which expressed themselves in certain distinctive habits and attitudes. These he had to change if his men were to be taken for 'Amis'; their clothes and the vehicles they drove wouldn't be enough to identify them as GIs. More was needed. Not only did his volunteers learn how to chew gum in the American fashion, but they also had to learn how to 'lounge', taking things casually, leaning against a wall, loosening their bodies up as the GIs did. Skorzeny reasoned that it was no use just dressing a soldier up in drab olive uniforms and giving him gum to chew just to have him spring to attention rigidly when an officer gave an order as if he were some old-fashioned Prussian guardsman.

But in his own post-war account of this strange exercise at Gräfenwöhr,

Skorzeny makes no reference to any specific training of his special 'jeep teams' of Captain Stielau's elite unit. Nor does he mention their specific objectives.*

Why? Was it because members of the Stielau outfit were already on the German border with Belgium and Luxembourg preparing for another kind of mission altogether?

In essence the whole area, Luxembourg and deep into what was called 'New Belgium', was German-speaking. 'New Belgium', consisting of three East Cantons of Eupen, Malmedy and St Vith, had been German until 1918 when the Treaty of Versailles ceded them to Belgium. Both Luxembourg and 'New Belgium' had become German again in 1940 and their male citizens were called up to the German Army. In addition many people on both sides of the Eifel-Ardennes border were related to each other and the terrain was definitely ideal for any agent who spoke the local patois.

It was not surprising that the locals later told Allied interrogators that they had been expecting the Germans to attack for most of that autumn of 1944. Germans, often disguised as Americans, had been spotted by the locals everywhere. At US VIII Corps Headquarters in Bastogne, the citizens were mostly French-speaking, but there was a large contingent of German refugees in the town, which would soon become the site of the famous siege. They reported Germans spotted laying out DZs for parachute drops. VIII Corps HQ was informed. But the citizens' warnings were pooh-poohed. American Intelligence officers thought the warning just another example of the traditional Belgian spy phobia.

Down in the Luxembourg front-line town of Clervaux, Headquarters of the 28th Division's ill-fated 110th Infantry Regiment, similar reports and rumours of German spies in US uniform, or dressed as farmers, were received. Once again they were dismissed as alarmist by the regiment's staff stationed above the town in the Hotel Clarvallis. The staff would soon think differently when two German secret radio operators, located in an empty *pharmacie* (it's still there), a couple of hundred yards away from the HQ, started bringing down artillery fire on the US positions.

But there was one place on that long frontier, where these mysterious figures were spotted by local farmers and peasants, which didn't seem important enough for a German to risk being shot as a spy if he were apprehended there.

This was the rural crossroads on the Belgian N-31 country road from Malmedy to Vielsalm. It ran through stretches of desolate forest past only

---

*The War Diary of the German High Command of that time is also extremely reticent on the whole subject of Skorzeny's formation, though it does state: 'So many difficulties arose from the insistence on preserving complete security that many members of the special group had to be released.' It would seem hardly likely that Skorzeny would let men go, who already knew something of this secret operation.

a handful of villages until it came to the one-horse hamlet of Poteau, directly on the linguistic border between French-speaking 'Old Belgium' and German-speaking 'New Belgium'. Here on one side of the road the locals were Walloons speaking French; on the other were the native speakers of the local German dialect.

More than once the French-speaking farmers encountered US officers or lone GIs who turned away from them when they realised the civilians were Walloons, though these strange Americans seemed quite at ease with the civilians who spoke German on the other side of the linguistic divide.

On one occasion, one of these Americans offered a local farmer a cigar. The latter accepted it with alacrity. Tobacco was hard to come by. Here and there the locals had grown their own, spraying the crumbling yellowed leaves with 'Virginia odour' to make the finished product halfway smokeable. But when the farmer came to smoke the 'American' cigar, he found it tasted just the same as his 'homemade' product. The cigar was German.

In particular, it seemed to the more curious of the locals (and in that area where the 'Old Belgian' maquis of the 'White Army' operated and there were these Franco-German mixed populations, it wasn't wise to be too curious), that these wandering Americans were interested in one point. It was the deeply wooded area between Poteau and the main road that led from Vielsalm and on across the hills to Huy and the other cities on the Meuse river which had bridges across the river, the last natural barrier before the plain of northern Belgium, the capital Brussels, and the great Allied supply port of Antwerp.

For some other reason, too, they asked the way to the 'French' or 'Napoleon Cross' in the woods, some 250 yards from the Poteau road. The locals couldn't guess why. What was so important about this weathered monument, dating back to the late 18th or early 19th century?

Later, when the Germans returned in December 1944, one of the locals who had encountered these 'Americans' was accosted by a German officer in SS uniform. The latter waved to him and asked cheerfully: 'Don't you remember me? I gave you a cigar.' It was then that the slow-witted farmer tumbled to it. The 'Napoleon Cross' provided a convenient landmark and rallying point between the two major road systems leading through the Ardennes to the Meuse river. But the chronicler of that time over sixty years ago now recorded that the farmer never asked, 'A rallying point for what . . . ?

The volunteers were puzzled, very puzzled. On all sides rumour upon rumour circulated in the isolated, now snowbound, Bavarian camp which held the men who would carry out 'Operation Grab'. There was talk of two men being executed for having revealed a 'great secret' in their letters home, which naturally were censored. According to the 'scuttlebutt', two Dutch truck drivers who had brought supplies to the camp had been imprisoned or even executed because they had later revealed details of what was going on at Gräfenwöhr.

Then there was wild talk about the objective of this 'Trojan Horse' operation. Some said that they were to attack across France to Lorient on the Brittany coast where a General Frambacher was still holding with the German garrison.* Others maintained that their mission was to be more complicated than that. They were actually going to attack Strasbourg, which had just fallen into Allied hands, recapture it and give it back to the Führer as a Christmas present.

At first, as Skorzeny stated after the war, he attempted to stop these 'latrine-o-grams'. He thought they were bad for the troops' morale. But in the end he realised that these wild rumours might well provide an excellent cover for the real operation. So he allowed his volunteers to whisper the most outrageous things to one another as they sat in their eight-seater 'thunderboxes' (hence the name 'latrine-o-gram'). For he knew his own spies among the troops would report any rumours that came close to the truth about his 150 Panzer Brigade, as it was now called, and the secret 'Stielau Company'.

Then, completely out of the blue, a rumour reached him personally: one that would plague him for years to come and one that hasn't been really scotched to this very day. Its cause and effect has remained one of the major mysteries of what has been called 'America's Gettysburg of the 20th century', i.e. the Battle of the Bulge.

According to Skorzeny's account (and again just as with his initial conversation with Hitler on 'Operation Grab', we have only his word on this), one morning his adjutant told him that a young officer, identified only as 'Leutnant N', requested permission to speak to the Commanding Officer. 'Leutnant N' was apparently a team leader in charge of a jeep in Captain Stielau's mysterious outfit.

Skorzeny, the man who had rescued Mussolini and kidnapped Horthy's son, was now no longer in the habit of giving his precious time to mere lieutenants. But in this case he relented and told his adjutant that he would see 'Leutnant N'.

So now 'under four eyes', as the German expression for a private conversation has it, 'Leutnant N' gushed excitedly: 'Obersturm, I think I know what the real objective is.'

Skorzeny recalled that he sat bolt-upright with shock at the young

---

*General Frambacher told the author that he finally decided to surrender, days after the official surrender of Germany to the Allies, when his quartermaster informed him there was no more sawdust from the local railway sleepers to mix with their meagre supply of flour to make bread for the troops.

man's announcement. Officially only he and two other officers at the camp knew what the real mission was. Had someone spilled the beans? But before Skorzeny could begin to bluster, 'Leutnant N' said: 'The Brigade is to march on Paris, sir . . . and capture Eisenhower's headquarters.'

With an effort, as Skorzeny recalled, he forced himself to adopt a non-committal manner. He frowned however as if he did not like what he heard. The look seemed to convince the young officer that he had guessed right.

With all the enthusiasm of youth, Leutnant N said:

> May I offer you my co-operation, sir? I was stationed in France for a long time and I know Paris well. My French is good too, You can rely on me, sir . . . This is my plan.

According to Skorzeny the eager young officer explained that the 150th Panzer Brigade would enter the French capital from different directions, posing as Americans. With them they would bring captured German tanks on transports and a bogus 'very important American general'. The pseudo-Americans would explain that these captured German tanks, which had new and secret features, were to be taken to the rear to be examined by ordnance experts.

'Leutnant N' went on to suggest that all the various 150 Brigades needed was a central rallying point. There they would concentrate and prepare for a daring raid on Eisenhower's headquarters at Versailles. The raid shouldn't be too difficult. Obviously the Amis wouldn't have any armour to speak of in Paris and they, the Germans, knew their way around Versailles. After all they had used the place themselves for four years during the Occupation.

As Skorzeny later described, he pretended to go along with the excited young officer's proposals. He told 'Leutnant N' that he, too, knew Paris well and had often sat in the Café de la Paix sipping a Ricard or Pernod, watching the world go by. Perhaps the world-famous café might serve as a rallying point. After the war Skorzeny would confess that he was 'to regret ever mentioning that damned Café de la Paix'.

After Skorzeny had warned the young officer not to let anyone else in on the great secret ('Don't mention it to anyone. When the time comes, I'll call on you.'), he dismissed him, knowing the secret wouldn't last the day. It didn't. Next day the Gräfenwöhr camp was buzzing with the latest hot rumour; they were going to kidnap Eisenhower. One of the first of the Stielau Company to be captured, 'Captain Murray Eddie O'Conner', in reality Peter Ackermann, told his captors before they shot him: 'At the end of ten days no one was in any doubt as to our objective. The officers' mess waiters passed on everything.' A new captive, Corporal Wilhelm Schmidt, also soon to be executed, reinforced Ackermann's story. He confessed:

'Our unit included a group of engineers whose job it was to destroy headquarters and kill the headquarters personnel.'

Thus, according to Skorzeny, the story of the attempted Eisenhower assassination was born, a figment of the imagination of an excited young officer. The events of that 20 November 1944, when Skorzeny maintained that celebrated interview took place, were later dismissed by the commando leader as 'a little stone which spread large ripples' and became 'evil propaganda . . . used by the enemy . . . to ensure that three years later I was to face a US military tribunal.'

But if that discussion really had taken place, why would Eisenhower later declare that Skorzeny was 'the most dangerous man in Europe' and have his portrait circulated throughout Allied Europe? The placard with Skorzeny's picture on it read: 'Wanted. Skorzeny . . . Spy, Saboteur' (and more relevant to our story) 'assassin'. In short, Eisenhower would virtually demand Skorzeny's head on a silver platter.

Looking at Skorzeny's own account, it seems unlikely that a very junior officer such as 'Leutnant N' would have dared approach a highly decorated colonel who had undertaken so many top level missions and had the ear of the Führer himself and then convince the Austrian giant that he could actually contribute to the plan: something which Skorzeny actually agreed to. It doesn't ring true, especially when Skorzeny was in trouble after his surrender on account of the alleged assassination attempt, and 'Leutnant N's' testimony would have been of great value to him. But no 'Leutnant N' was to be found and never would be. In other words, did the excitable young officer really exist?

In Sheen's Counter-Intelligence Summary, written ten days after that supposed Skorzeny-Leutnant N meeting, on 1 December 1944, there was the warning that: 'Captured saboteurs emphasise impressive scale of Skorzeny's plan for sabotage and subversion. He . . . has created certain new units apparently for para-military use.' This formation, Eisenhower's chief-of-staff and the officer who really ran the Supreme Headquarters passed on to his boss at the morning Versailles staff conference.

It seems, therefore, that some officers at the Supreme HQ were already taking the Skorzeny threat seriously nearly *two* weeks before the Battle of the Bulge, and prisoners from the Stielau Company began revealing the details of the plot to kill the Supreme Commander with these 'para-military' formations.

So what do we make of Skorzeny's mysterious 'Leutnant N' who first broached the Eisenhower murder plan: an officer who made one short appearance on the stage of history only to disappear completely thereafter. Or the threat posed by the 'Skorzeny killers', as they would be known later to the world? That threat was seemingly known to Sheen and counter-intelligence before the Battle of the Bulge. Why, too, would both sides, Skorzeny and Sheen, pooh-pooh the whole idea of an attempted assassination of the Supreme Commander, with Sheen declaring after Skorzeny had surrendered in May '45 that it was a 'hoax'? Skorzeny, for his part, as we have seen, blamed everything on the rumour started and then circulated by the mysterious 'Leutnant N'. Even when Skorzeny had been freed and was apparently no longer under pressure from his one-time American captors, the commando leader repeated the story in his memoirs. A lot of questions with few answers.

Do we then accept both the American and German versions of Skorzeny's role as that of a reconnaissance and sabotage mission, which as the Americans put it, so confused the American defenders that 'half a million GIs [were] playing cat and mouse with each other every time they met.*

And finally, what do we make of Skorzeny's statement immediately after his surrender to the Americans and before he had been interviewed by Colonel Sheen (posing incidently as another officer altogether), 'if I had wanted to kill Eisenhower I would have done so . . .'?

Now, the time of rumour and counter-rumour was over in Gräfenwöhr. The 150th Panzer Brigade and the Stielau Company were as trained for their mission as they ever would be. They had learned the latest recognition signals: blue lights during daylight, red at night; an unbuttoned second tunic button; a particular way of tilting their helmets; particular letters on the sides of their American vehicles (always on the left), such as 'C', 'D', 'X' and 'Z'.

In this way the undercover soldiers could work together with the men of Obersturmbannführer Peiper's 1st SS Battle Group, which would lead the way in the coming battle for Dietrich's 6th SS Panzer Army so that the SS would have the honour of reaching their objectives before von Manteuffel's 5th Panzer Army from the Wehrmacht.

So on 12 December 1944 they started to ship out from Bavaria to their jump-off positions in the German Eifel to the north. The troop trains Skorzeny's men used followed circuitous routes and moved only by night. By day these trains were shunted into camouflaged sidings where the men camped out and were 'protected' by the local Gestapo. At this stage of the operation Skorzeny was taking no chances; the Gestapo was there to prevent anyone from deserting.

Finally after the long freezing journeys, the 150 Brigade was concentrated in the Munstereifel-Stadtkyll area of the Eifel where the 6th SS Panzer Army was already forming ready for the attack across the nearby German-Belgian border. Here they were issued with US Army paybooks and driving licences though there weren't any American dogtags available for them: an unfortunate oversight.

*General Bradley, 12th US Army Group Commander.

Unknown to the rest of 150 Brigade, the Stielau Company had taken a separate route from Gräfenwöhr, being sent to Wahn Airport just outside Cologne. It was from here that the last German mass para-drop of WWII was launched – Colonel von der Heydte's 1,200-strong force aimed at stopping US reinforcements reaching the battlefield from the north. Was it just a coincidence that Skorzeny's most powerful formation of English-speaking troops was stationed next to an operational airfield? At all events those 'jeep teams' which did reach the 150th Brigade's and the 1st SS's final assembly areas in the Blankenheim Forest just opposite the 'Lozheim Gap' through which they would drive into Belgium, were kept segregated from their SS comrades while they waited for the signal to attack.

As Sergeant Heinz Rohde, one of the jeep teams, recalled in 1950: 'When we arrived in a raging snowstorm, several grinning officers appeared and before our tired eyes proceeded to open several sealed cans.'

And what cans they were! 'The first one cheered us up no end . . . It was packed to the top with Ami cigarettes, chocolates, coffee, matches and cans of food of all kinds.'

According to Rohde, these cans were shared out among his suddenly happy comrades 'with Prussian fairness' and the next case was then opened. It was intended for Rohde's sole use as team leader. It was to make 'sure we didn't lack for anything during our mission. For it was packed with US dollars, English pounds etc.' There were also huge numbers of French and Belgian francs, to be used to bribe French and Belgian dockers at key coastal supply ports, in particular Antwerp, to go on strike. The strike would coincide with the Sixth Panzer Army's drive for the Franco-Belgian coast and would paralyse shipping being used to bring in Allied supplies and reinforcements.

What a happy Rohde and the rest of his team didn't know on that snowy day in the Eifel forest was that all the foreign notes were clever forgeries, manufactured by professional crooks, some of them imprisoned Jews, working from German concentration camps.

But the last case to be presented to the Stielau men by the SS officer messengers killed their happy mood immediately when they learned of its contents:

> It offered a sight of numerous cigarette lighters of the kind the Amis called the 'zippo'. At first there seemed nothing special about these lighters. They were cheap metal, mass-produced items with no particularly exclusive features. That was until a grinning SS major told us what they were for. He pointed out that the glass tube, instead of containing lighter fuel, was filled with cyanide. All we needed to do if we were caught was to bite into the tube and all our problems would be solved. *Guten Appetit*!

That put an end to the team's happy mood.

> So we trailed back to our wigwams [Rohde meant their tents]. For the first time since we had joined Skorzeny, we realised what we had let ourselves in for on 'Ascension Day Commando' [a one-time journey to heaven, i.e. a suicide mission].

CHAPTER III
The Last Assault

According to Skorzeny's own account, he arrived in the Eifel and set up his headquarters in a modest house in the small town of Schmidtheim. On the Thursday before the start of the offensive on the following Saturday, 16 December 1944, he took part in the last-minute discussions of the senior officers of 6th SS Panzer Army. There his role in the coming attack was explained and he learned that, as soon as Peiper had broken through the US 99th Division in the Losheim Gap and the US 14th Cavalry Group which provided the link between that division and the US 166th Infantry Division, his 150th Panzer Division would pass through Peiper's point and lead the way to the Meuse bridges. Little mention was made of Skorzeny's jeep teams save that the SS were told how to recognise these ill-fated soldiers dressed in US uniforms. In the main the recognition signal would be the letter 'Z' on the sides of the 150th's vehicles. This was raised so that the SS could trace the letter in the darkness.

Then began the long nervous wait for the offensive to commence. Peiper's SS veterans, arrogant warriors who had been fighting since 1939, were not particularly interested in Skorzeny's covert operations. They were too concerned with what was to come, events that would give them a place in the history of WWII, but not one they – those who survived – would be proud of. For it would be accompanied by a smear on their military honour that they would never be able to eradicate until they finally passed away as bitter, forsaken old men, shunned even by their own children.

Thus it is that we hear virtually nothing of Skorzeny in those forty-eight hours that were left before dawn on the coming Saturday. Nor have the few of his deep teams who survived anything to say about their commander during that period. Skorzeny does not seem to have visited them in their 'wigwams' and so we know little of what his intentions were. Indeed Rohde and his men, who would be heading into the unknown the day before the counter-offensive start, were inspected only once by a dashing young tank officer in the black uniform of the 12th SS Panzer Division, 'the Hitler Youth'. Five years later, Rohde reported:

> He inspected us without asking any questions about our mission. All he did was shake his head, as if he couldn't believe what he was seeing. Then we were off, heading for a circle of trees, which marked the narrow strip of no-man's land.

The first jeep team attached to the 6th SS Panzer Army was on its way into the dangerous unknown. As Heinz Rohde commented later: 'Nobody bothered to say *Auf wiedersehen*'.

Rohde need not have worried unduly, for once the jeep team had penetrated the thin shell of the US 99th Infantry Division, a relatively raw division in the area, there was little to stop them. The rear was virtually devoid of American troops and what there were were mostly coloured supply units and workshops.

For on 2 December Colonel 'Monk' Dickson, the opposing US 1st Army's Chief-of-Intelligence, had reported on Skorzeny's operation order and the routes laid down for his columns. Eight days later Dickson repeated the information in another report (these reports were naturally passed on to Colonel Sheen and his boss, General Strong). But nothing was done about them.

Then events proved that despite all this detailed information, SHAEF didn't really believe in either a German counter-offensive or the operation. The only people who were beginning to worry were Sheen and his CIC operatives. Then their jobs were at stake. Still, as we have seen, Sheen, forced out of the States by FDR and low man on the totem pole in Versailles, was not the man to make the bosses sit up and take notice.

Admittedly the British evacuated the population from the Roer area near the German frontier in Holland and the French set up a line of checkpoints between Givet and Vise, forbidding all civilian journeys longer than four kilometres. But these were authoritarian countries, used to taking a heavy hand with civilians. The Americans had done little to evacuate German civilians from their area of the Eifel.

Indeed both the British and Americans were more concerned, it seemed, with subversive activity in neighbouring Allied countries such as France with its large communist party, and Belgium with 70,000 members of the resistance, the 'White Army', still under arms, than with the enemy. As Bradley's staff put it in their final report of the campaign:

> No evidence of operations by subversive organisations in liberated countries was encountered. Perhaps the most serious threat to Allied security in this respect came from the resistance groups in Belgium which remained active and retained their arms in defiance of

government decree.* Soon the Americans would learn just how wrong their estimates had been.

At precisely 05.30 hours on the morning of Saturday 16 December 1944, two thousand German guns of all calibres crashed into ear-splitting activity. All along the eighty-mile Eifel-Ardennes front they opened up. At the towns such as St Vith, just behind what had been called hitherto 'the Ghost Front', because nothing had happened there for the last three months, the 14-inch shells came slamming down to alert the terrified Belgian townsfolk and their US liberators that the Germans were coming back.

An eruption of flame and smoke burst all along that lonely front, where US divisions had been sent to acquire experience or to recuperate after combat, continued for exactly half an hour. Then as abruptly and as startlingly as it had started, the bombardment ceased. There was a loud, echoing silence. In their foxholes and bunkers the shaken GIs raised their heads and stared ahead of them. In the townships and villages the civilians did the same. What was going on? What were the Germans up to this time? Those local civilians not in the know soon found out.

At 0600 hours the first white-clad German infantry came out of the snow-heavy firs to attack the positions of the 106th, the 14th Cavalry and the 99th Infantry. American resistance crumbled swiftly. The first six fortified villages were taken. But US resistance on the German right flank, where the Sixth Panzer Army was to break through, was stronger than General Dietrich and that 'arrogant swine' Peiper (as the General always called his subordinate behind his back) had anticipated. The German assault infantry division, the 3rd Fallschirmjägerdivision, was only a little more experienced than the US 99th Infantry which it was attacking and the parachutists, who had never seen an aeroplane from the inside, were suffering too many casualties and taking too much time to take their objectives.

Back on the German side of the Losheim Gap, Dietrich and Peiper fumed. Already they were behind schedule. Peiper, 31 years old and Hitler's favourite SS armoured commander, tried to force his way through by brute force, sweeping aside all obstacles even when they were his own tanks blown up by enemy mines. Behind him waiting to let loose his 15th Panzer Brigade, Skorzeny seemed to be losing faith in the offensive already.

By noon that embattled Saturday, he gave up trying to reach the head of the stalled German tank column himself and returned to his village HQ.

---

*In November 1944 the British were forced to secretly surround the Belgian capital with a whole division, the 11th Armoured, just in case a rebellion broke out there as it had done in Greece.

Everywhere he had seen violent fighting, but little progress. 'The intended collapse of the whole front, 'he wrote later, 'had not been achieved.' Indeed, as he said himself, he was already considering whether 'Operation Grab', or at least the 150th Brigade's role in it, should be called off. After all, the success of the whole operation had depended upon a swift and clean breakthrough. In the end he decided to wait another twenty-four hours before making a final decision.

After a brief nap that afternoon, he spent the rest of the day talking to newly captured US POWs, who assured him they had been caught completely off guard by the attack. That reassured him somewhat. As did his brief conversation with one of his teams, made up of English-speaking Marines, who radiated confidence and enthusiasm. Then he decided to sleep again in the hope that the new day, Sunday 17th, would bring a complete breakthrough. He fell asleep again, wondering, as he wrote afterwards, what had happened to his seven jeep teams that had already crossed and penetrated the Ami frontline.

While Skorzeny slept that Saturday in the little white-washed cottage in Schmidtheim, Stielau's men were already at work in Belgium and Luxembourg. The leader of one team succeeded in misleading a whole regiment from the 'Big Red One', the famed US 1st Infantry Division, coming down to the north to help bolster up the side of the 'Bulge' which was already beginning to develop. Another team stopped by a US armoured column simulated terror so convincingly, crying the 'Krauts are coming!', that American Shermans turned and fled in terror. Another pulled off an even greater coup. The four-man jeep team succeeded in cutting the main cable linking General Hodges, commander of the US 1st Army, and his boss General Bradley. Now the two senior commanders at Spa, Belgium and Luxembourg City were unable to talk with one another directly.

Sergeant Rohde and his jeep team were, however, the only group that reported almost immediately to give Skorzeny a detailed account of what things were like behind the crumbling US front and on towards the great natural barrier, the Meuse river.

Rohde had started out at just the right time. Everywhere the disguised Germans encountered fleeing, sometimes panic-stricken GIs. They were the rearline outfits and also frontline ones trying to escape the on-coming Germans, crying 'the Krauts are coming . . . the Krauts are right behind us . . .'. Under such circumstances no one was taking any notice of the Rohde jeep team.

But there was a hitch. To his horror, the sergeant saw the Americans were driving with their headlights full on, while his were still blacked-out. In that bumper-to-bumper traffic Rohde knew there was no stopping. So pretending they had engine trouble, he and his driver pushed the jeep to the side of the packed road.

Under the cover of a hood, they pretended to work on the motor, and at the same time removed the blackout from the headlights, only to hear a jeep roll to a stop behind them. As Rohde described it:

> A captain raised his long legs over the side of the jeep and came towards us. In a deep voice he asked if he should tow us to the next motor transport outfit.

That frightened the disguised NCO. But the driver reacted first. He got behind the steering wheel, turned the key and the jeep started first time. Rohde thanked the captain, breathed a sign of relief and started rolling westwards once more.

Later that day, the Rohde team reached the bridge across the Meuse at the medieval town of Huy. What he found there would later please Skorzeny. By the lights of the vehicles fleeing across the bridge, the watching Germans could see that the bridge was lightly guarded. As he recalled afterwards Rohde could make out

> . . . there were a number of typical Ami tents on the eastern bank. From them soldiers came and went all the time. Obviously they belonged to a guard company responsible for the bridge. Now we could see, too, the Americans positioning a searchlight on the other side of the river. Had they got wind of our mission?*

Rohde need not have worried. They hadn't been spotted and soon he realised that the guard company, if that was what it was, was armed only with handguns; nothing that would stop the German armour, still waiting to roll towards the Meuse.

Still that information didn't help either Peiper or Rohde's boss Obersturmbannführer Skorzeny. His Brigade was stalled and he was not receiving the information he needed from all his jeep teams. So far only a few had reported back. Where were they and what were they up to? Little did the impatient commando leader know that – accidentally – one of the teams was going to achieve the greatest psychological warfare victory of the Battle of the Bulge that very day, Sunday 17 December 1944.

By now fear and tension raged throughout eastern Belgium, indeed as far as the bigger cities of the west, Brussels, Louvain, Mechelen and the like. The Germans were on their way back. Undoubtedly they'd pay off old scores. The Gestapo, as always, would know everything. The resistance men of the 'White Army', who had been so full of themselves only the

---

*If there had been a US guard company there, it soon vanished, later to be replaced by hastily whistled up men of the SAS and the British 29th Armoured Brigade.

month before, took off their uniforms, buried their weapons and faded quietly into the background. The portraits of Churchill and Roosevelt which had decorated virtually every house window were swiftly removed. Civilians, such as black marketeers, who were known to have extensive dealings with Anglo-American soldiers, were shunned. Even the good-time girls, who sold their bodies to servicemen behind Liège's main station or the Rue Neuve just off Brussels' 'Bon Marché', disappeared from the scene.

Now every crossroads and bridge in the rear areas was guarded by hurriedly assembled teams of British, American, French and Belgian soldiers. Montgomery was rushing up elements of 30 Corps from the Belgian interior and Holland to guard the Meuse bridges and, if necessary, make a last stand on the great river line.

With an estimated fifty-six German columns now breaking loose in the Ardennes, it was understandable that the defenders of those bridges and crossroads, waiting in the freezing cold, were nervous and jumpy. At any minute German tanks might appear from the east and what would they be able to do with their handguns against the massive Tigers and Panthers?

The mood was no different at the bridge in the small Belgian town of Aywaille south of Liège and twelve miles from a bridge across the Meuse itself at Englis. There was a small force of US military policemen there – 'snowdrops' the locals called them – and a handful of black service troops, who had just been armed and were pretty jumpy. As Brigadier Essame of the British 43rd Infantry Division commented later, one had to be pretty careful with US coloured troops 'because they had already shot one American and two Belgians'.

According to the future Docteur Maquet, a 16-year-old local boy who was friendly with the US MP who normally guarded the town's bridge, about midday on Sunday 17 December, a jeep was spotted down the cobbled 18th-century street which led to the local bridge. It contained three men in GI uniform. One of the MPs raised his right hand. The jeep braked. There was a small exchange in English. Then one of the 'snowdrops' asked for the password. As young Paul Maquet heard later from his friend, the US military policemen, the jeep driver 'paled and looked worried'.

The jeep driver blustered that he hadn't been given one. But the MP knew that all soldiers in the Liège area of the COMZ who were travelling that day *had* been given one with their trip ticket.

Swiftly the three men in the jeep had their identities secured. They were PFC George Senzenbach, PFC Clarence W Lawrence and PFC Clarence van de Zerth. Nothing special about that. But while the men's identities were being checked, others at the bridge roadblock started to search the jeep.

The searchers struck gold almost immediately. These were no ordinary

GIs, that was for certain. In the rear, hidden under the seat, they discovered a huge roll of hundred dollar bills, as fresh as they came from the printing press, the product naturally of the concentration camp forgers.

For a while the searchers thought they had encountered some pretty successful GI black marketeers. But soon they dug up from the interior of the jeep two British sten guns, two Colts, two German Walther pistols, plastic explosive and, most incriminating of all, a radio transmitter of German origin. Shortly afterwards, they discovered the zippo lighters, containing the 'L' pills.

Now, thoroughly frightened, the smallest of the three began to sing. His name was not George Senzenbach, but Wilhelm Schmidt and he was a corporal in the German Army. It was a sensation that freezing Sunday afternoon, as the crowd of shabby civilians stared at the prisoners as if they had just dropped in from outer space. Schmidt explained that he and his comrades had set off from the pretty German border town of Monschau on 12 December. According to the little corporal, it had taken them five days to penetrate the US lines, though the distance between Monschau and Aywaille was less than fifty miles. (Perhaps he was lying. We don't know: Schmidt didn't live long enough to be forthcoming on why it had taken them so long to get to the Belgian town.)

As Schmidt told it, they had posed as members of the US 5th Armored Division and had 'reported on the Meuse bridges and the roads leading to those bridges'.

The senior NCO didn't wait to hear any more. He raced for the nearest phone and made contact with Military Police HQ in Liège. His call must have startled the people at the other end for within a matter of thirty minutes or so a fleet of jeeps, containing heavily armed 'white mice' and members of the CIC of all ranks, came racing down the grey, cobbled streets of Aywaille, past the church and on to the bridge where the prisoners waited for them. The Top Brass was obviously very eager to hear the story of the three crestfallen Germans who would never see their homeland again.

It is not known what methods the impatient CIC men used on the prisoners to make them talk so fast. US Intelligence was not too squeamish with their prisoners at the best of times. After all, back home where most of the CIC agents had been policemen in civilian life, 'third degree methods' were still commonplace and the Top Brass was screaming for information. So they made the Germans talk and what a tale they had to tell!

Schmidt, who had been one of the first volunteers to join Skorzeny, told his interrogators:

> Early in November I reported to an SS camp at Friedenthal, where I was examined as to my linguistic ability by a board consisting of an

SS, a Luftwaffe and a naval officer. I passed the test. But I was ordered to refresh my English. For this purpose I spent three weeks at prisoner-of-war camps in Kuestrin and Limburg where large numbers of American prisoners were being held.

Later Schmidt, now chain-smoking American cigarettes given to him by his interrogators as a reward for spilling the beans, explained how he had been trained at Gräfenwöhr before adding that he and his group had been given the task of 'destroying headquarters and headquarters personnel'.

'What ... what headquarters and what personnel?' he was asked urgently.

Now all those wild rumours which had circulated in Gräfenwöhr the month before came out: the dash across France to relieve the German-held port of Lorient; the surprise attack on Montgomery's forward HQ, a collection of poorly defended caravans in rural Holland, the transporting of the two captured Tiger tanks by the assassins to the rendezvous in Paris's Café de la Paix.

'To do what?' one of the CIC men asked sharply.

'To kill General Eisenhower,' came the sensational reply.

The three pseudo-Americans had served their purpose. They were court-martialled five days later and shot on 22 December at Henri-la-Chapelle, just outside Aachen.*

Before sentence was carried out, they appealed for mercy to the commander of the US 1st Army, General Hodges, who was in a state of nervous breakdown himself and in no mood to be lenient:

> We have been captured by the Americans without having fired a single shot because we did not wish to become murderers. We were sentenced to death and are now dying for criminals, who have not only us, but also – and that is worse – our families on their conscience.

It is said that the three men asked for German Christmas carols to be sung on their last night on earth. A group of German female auxiliaries also in prison obliged them and thus they prepared for death to the tune of '*Stille Nacht, Heilige Nacht*', composed by that obscure Austrian village priest, whose fellow Austrian Skorzeny who was one of those 'criminals' for whom they were soon to die.

Now there were sightings of 'Skorzeny's killers', real or imagined, everywhere. At Poteau, where strange 'Americans' had been sighted by the locals long before the great counter-attack started, a group of 'Americans' appeared riding on self-propelled guns. They passed a real

---

*Although the wall against which they were shot is hidden today, the bullet marks left by the US firing squad can still be seen on it.

American sergeant who thought the GIs' boots looked 'funny'. Before the NCO from the 32nd Squadron of the 14th Cavalry Group could challenge the newcomers, one of them cried, 'We're E Company!'.

That was enough for the suspicious sergeant. In the cavalry there were no companies, only 'squadrons', or in the case of smaller units 'troops'. He opened fire and the pseudo-Americans of Skorzeny's Stielau Company died on the spot.

But not all of the jeep teams died or were captured. Few as they were, they caused a tremendous spy-and-sabotage scare throughout France and Belgium. Radio Calais, the Allied propaganda station run by journalist Sefton Delmer, which was aimed at undermining the fighting spirit of the German Army, reported that some 250 men of Skorzeny's commandos in US uniform had been captured. Later, when Skorzeny received the report, he laughed out loud. As he didn't have that many men in the field, he reasoned that the Amis must have mistakenly arrested some of their own men. Indeed when he himself was an American prisoner, he met a US captain who was apprehended because he was wearing looted German jackboots. Another two guards told him that they had been put in jail as 'Kraut spies' because they had remarked while eating in a strange mess that the 'chow' was good. Obviously that had been a very suspect remark to make about the fare produced by the GI cooks.

GIs and generals, they all faced questioning by their own comrades and fellow officers as the spy scare, set off by Skorzeny, grew ever wilder. Montgomery had the tyres of his car shot out. Thereafter he drove with a large Union flag adorning his old-fashioned Rolls-Royce and demanded US identification from Eisenhower. General Bradley was stopped time and time again by GIs asking him trick questions to check whether he was really an American. Twice he got the answers wrong, but it didn't seem to matter; the GIs who interrogated the general didn't know the real answers themselves. Soon, however, the 12th Army Group Commander wouldn't be travelling far at all. The threat of assassination kept him in virtual hiding at the Hotel Alfa, Luxembourg City, where he had located his headquarters in the centre of that city. There Bradley slept in a different bedroom every night and left the hotel through the kitchen and the back door. The bright general's stars were removed from his helmet as they were from his sedan. Once when the hotel manager warned the three-star army group commander to keep away from the hotel's front windows, Bradley asked why. 'Because,' the manager explained, pointing to the exit to Luxembourg's main station opposite the Hotel HQ, 'a sniper could get you easily from over there, General', Bradley jumped back hastily and never went near the window again.

General Hodges of the US 1st Army had already fled his HQ at Spa, leaving top secret documents unburnt everywhere, and moved to Châteaufontaine where his staff excused his flight and condition by saying he was suffering from viral pneumonia (in fact he had taken to his bed, unable to act, with a blanket thrown over his skinny shoulders*). He wrote about the activities of Skorzeny's men: 'These men are completely ruthless and prepared to sacrifice their lives.' Armed with explosives, he wrote in his diary, some of them possess a new type of hand grenade fired from a pistol. He added: 'All personnel speak fluent English.'

Alarmed even more by the findings of his intelligence officers after they had interrogated another group of captured 'Skorzeny Killers', he decided to warn Supreme Headquarters of the acute danger now facing the Top Brass there. For the captured men had told their captors:

> Skorzeny is on his way to Versailles to assassinate Eisenhower. He is travelling in an American ambulance full of fake wounded. He is to meet German agents at the Café de la Paix in Paris and they will give him final details of the security arrangements around Supreme Headquarters. Other American generals will be kidnapped.

This Hodges did by a top secret signal, which was followed the same day – 20 December 1944 – by one from Bradley's HQ addressed to Group Captain Jones who had incidentally warned Strong of the coming Ardennes Offensive in October. Jones of Bletchley Park was given a summary of Hodges' signal and informed that the Skorzeny agents will 'attempt to assassinate SHAEF and other high officials'.

One of those 'other high officials' could only be the Supreme Commander himself. The great flap in Versailles could now commence.

The cynical Major Noel Annan of Strong's Intelligence section at Versailles was there that Sunday afternoon when it all started. The staff were working flat out. Reports of new German units appearing in the enemy's Order-of-Battle in the Ardennes were coming in all the time. Already the Intelligence staff officers had identified fifteen German divisions and estimated that there were at least fifty German columns at loose in the forests of the German-Belgian Eifel-Ardennes region.

Then, while the phones jangled, the typewriters clattered and staff officers hurried back and forth with their important gold folders and files, Colonel Sheen burst into Annan's room at the Hôtel Trianon crying, 'Skorzeny's on Paris!'

Somewhere outside, Sergeant Mickey McKeogh, ex-bellhop and now Eisenhower's loyal 'striker', heard the fuss and later described the 'security boys' i.e. Sheen and his sergeants, 'as scared . . . really scared'.

---

*Communicated to the author by Sir Carol Mather, then an SAS officer and one of Montgomery's 'eyes-and-ears', who acted as go-between for Montgomery and Hodges at that time.

They were. Now Sheen got the ear of General Strong himself, busy as he was with the new offensive he had so stubbornly refused to believe possible. Although it was Sheen himself who later took the blame for the 'great flap' of that last week of December '44, according to Annan it was Strong, the 'Hangman's Dilemma', who persuaded Eisenhower 'to incarcerate himself near his headquarters, surrounded by bodyguards of armoured vehicles'.

Later, Strong laid the blame for what happened thereafter on Sheen. He wrote that the story (of the Skorzeny killers) was too circumstantial to be ignored and instituted all manner of security precautions, to which 'Eisenhower agreed most reluctantly'.

Now things moved fast. Eisenhower was persuaded to leave his insecure villa and move closer to the Versailles HQ. Immediately Eisenhower became a prisoner in his own headquarters, cut off from the decision-making process. As Annan remarked later, it was unfortunate for it 'was the moment when Eisenhower should have been on the move to see Montgomery and Bradley and their army commanders'. Indeed during the whole of the Battle of the Bulge, it was only Montgomery and to a lesser extent Patton who visited the men doing the fighting; Eisenhower, Bradley and Hodges never did.

Kay Summersby, imprisoned in the HQ with Eisenhower, described the situation:

> Security officers immediately turned headquarters compound into a virtual fortress. Barbed wire appeared. Several tanks moved in. The normal guard was doubled, trebled, quadrupled. The pass system became a matter of life or death, instead of the old formality. The sound of car exhaust was enough to halt work in every office, to start a flurry of telephone calls to our office to enquire whether the boss was all right. The atmosphere was worse than that of a combat headquarters at the front, where everyone knows how to take such situations in their stride.

Once, according to Kay Summersby, Eisenhower grew so angry at the restriction that he snapped at her, 'Hell's fire, I'm going for a walk. If anyone wants to shoot me, he can go right ahead. I've got to get out. 'And walk he did, followed by a whole company, some 100 men, of heavily armed, suspicious military policemen. Even when he went to eat, he was taken to the mess hall in a Sherman tank!'

Sleep seemed impossible. As Kay Summersby remembered: 'I lay awake for hours and envisioning death – and worse at the hands of SS agents – with the tramp, tramp of heavy booted guards outside patrolling the tin roof.'

Captain Butcher, former vice-president of CBS Radio and Eisenhower's

PR man, was allowed in to see the Supreme Commander in that first week of the German offensive. He told his boss he had been stopped time and time again at roadblocks to have his ID checked. Butcher could see Eisenhower was in a bad mood and he knew why. There were guards everywhere and worried staff officers fussing around, checking up on Eisenhower's safety. Just before he left, he said, knowing that among the Top Brass it was an open secret that the Supreme Commander had been approached to run for President when Roosevelt completed his third term: 'Now you know how it feels to be a President and always under the watchful eye of the Secret Service.' Eisenhower wasn't amused, but one wonders if eight years later when Eisenhower really was President of the United States he remembered that quip made at the tense low point of his military career?

The tension rose and rose. In Paris, according to Strong:

> There was said to be something akin to panic. The French police were reporting the landing of parachutists near Supreme Headquarters, some of them dressed as priests and nuns – paratroops *always* seemed to disguise themselves as nuns and priests.

In Nice, Radio Nice reported that Skorzeny's para-agents had held up a local bank some four hundred miles away from the scene of the battle! The London *Daily Telegraph* informed its readers that specially trained female agents had been dropped in the vicinity of Paris. Their task was to seduce unwary GIs. Once the latter had been duly seduced and had 'revealed all' they were to be killed by a 'handy little dagger' that all these German Mata Haris carried in their purses.

A trap was set at the now infamous Café de la Paix. It failed to nab any Skorzeny agents. All it succeeded in doing was to apprehend two unfortunate American officers found breaking the curfew. A double was appointed. He was said to look like the Supreme Commander. Daily he would journey in the Supreme Commander's normal armoured staff car from the villa to Supreme HQ as he continued to do way into the New Year by which time the 'big flap' was over. He was rewarded much later for his 'bravery' with the command of an infantry regiment.

According to Strong, Eisenhower believed that the whole plot 'was greatly exaggerated' when told that his staff 'had complete and positive proof of such a plot'. He said that he would 'consider it miraculous if any German murderer could determine in advance that he could find his prospective victim on a particular railway train at a given moment at a given spot in Europe.'

Still Strong, now supporting the harassed Sheen, whose big moment this all was, was adamant. Although he personally didn't want to take responsibility of having the Supreme Commander locked up in his HQ at this critical period, 'it was difficult to place the responsibility on any one person', he felt he couldn't let Eisenhower loose. As he wrote afterwards:

> If anything had by chance happened to the Supreme Commander because insufficient precautions had been taken to protect him, the resulting chaos would have been disastrous. Eisenhower was not expendable.

But for the time being, Skorzeny knew nothing of what was happening in Versailles, where he and his 'killers' were supposed to be such a threat. On the day after Eisenhower was placed under a kind of 'house arrest', he was fully engaged with his 150 Panzer Brigade in attempting to capture the Belgian town of Malmedy. The town had already entered the history of the Battle of the Bulge as the site of the infamous 'Massacre of Malmedy'* which had taken place only a day or so before. Now the place was being held by a mixed bunch of US engineers and infantry. Skorzeny was to attack for the second time. This time his tanks would come in from both flanks. But, unknown to him, one of his disguised commandos had already been captured by the men of the 30th US Infantry Division. They had given their prisoner a hard time, threatening to shoot him as a spy. The German had started to sing. He told them – wrongly – that they were standing in the path of a whole SS Panzer Corps. He did tell the truth when he confessed that Malmedy itself was to be attacked by a panzer brigade – Skorzeny's.

Overnight Skorzeny's panzers rolled into their jump-off positions. One of the tanks, commanded by a Lieutenant Peter Mundt, now garbed as a corporal in the US Army, was a Panther which had been poorly disguised as an American tank.

Mundt was not particularly worried that the Panther didn't look very much like an American vehicle. He was a veteran of nearly three years in Russia. He was used to the worst and didn't expect this attack to be any better than the others he had taken part in. As he explained afterwards: 'We knew we were going to lose the war and regarded battle as some kind of lottery with the big prize – *survival!*'

Now Mundt's disguised Panther was in a hull-down position 100 yards away from Malmedy's viaduct station. To pass the time while they waited for the signal for the assault, Mundt ordered his radio man to tune to the British propaganda station Soldatensender Calais. The station was always good for the latest tunes, mild pornography and tittle-tattle about senior German officers.

However this December night, Soldatensender Calais was not at all

---

*The site of the 'massacre' was actually at the hilltop crossroads above Malmedy at a hamlet called Baugnez.

amusing. Suddenly the dance music stopped and a harsh voice barked in German, 'take aim – *fire.*' Another speaker took up the programme with '*Mit diesen Salven endete ein weiteres Erschiessenkommando Skorzenys*' ('With these volleys another one of Skorzeny's commando teams met its end'.) Three of Skorzeny's jeep teams had just been shot dead at Henri-Chapelle, only a matter of miles from where Mundt's tank was concealed at that very moment.

A mood of profound gloom descended upon the men waiting in the freezing cold for the attack to begin. It was not surprising that when the news of what had just happened at Henri-Chapelle that night spread, Skorzeny's men lost heart. Faced with stiff resistance the Germans failed to take Malmedy for a second time.

Still encarcerated in his headquarters prison, together with Kay Summersby, who noted, '[it] makes him mad' to be locked up like that, Eisenhower managed to write to his ever-complaining wife Mamie in the far-off United States. As Summersby recorded, he wrote:

> There are many things about this war that cannot be told now – possibly never – but they should make interesting talk between you and me when we're sitting in the sun, taking our elegant ease.*

Up on the heights above Malmedy, a gloomy, frustrated Skorzeny would not have shared that sentiment after the failure of the second attack. He'd never sit in the sun now 'taking [his] elegant ease'. He could already guess what might happen to him if and when Germany lost the war, and it would not involve a long and peaceful retirement. Still the commando leader did know things about the war and its personalities that couldn't be told then, perhaps never. In his particular case, if he did talk about them, especially what had happened and had been planned for this December, his life might well be in danger.

Watching the stragglers of the failed second attack come back up the hill, bringing their wounded with them, and on past the divisional HQ at the one-time internationally famed Hôtel du Moulin at Engelsdorf ('the village of Angels'),** Skorzeny must have felt a sense of failure. The men looked totally dispirited and beaten. Skorzeny knew there could be no third attack. Malmedy would remain in American hands. Everything seemed to have gone wrong. All their efforts and enthusiasm had been for nothing.

Later Skorzeny was walking over to the hotel, which had been the

---

*If several sources are to be believed, Eisenhower was not intending to go back to his Mamie. Instead he wanted to marry Kay Summersby. It is recorded when he told his boss, General Marshall, this, the latter threatened to 'hound him to the ends of the earth', if he did.
**Today the village bears the French name of Ligneuville.

headquarters of the 49th US Anti-Aircraft Brigade under a General Timberlake who had narrowly avoided capture by Peiper's Battle Group, when he heard the howl of heavy artillery.

Monsieur Peter Rupp, the 70-year-old Swiss owner of the hotel saw how the big Colonel staggered and seemed to fall as the fist-sized pieces of hot shrapnel hissed through the air. In fact Skorzeny had been hit in the face and blood was now pouring down his cheek. A soldier ran out to help the Colonel. Skorzeny waved him away almost angrily. He staggered into the hotel and seized a glass of cognac from the supplies left behind by General Timberlake four days before.

Downing it, Skorzeny asked the little hotel owner for a mirror to look at his face.* In his memoirs he recorded his feelings at that moment:

> I felt how the blood ran warmly down my cheek. Carefully I felt my face with my hand. Above my eye a lump of flesh was missing from my forehead and was hanging down over the eye. I was shocked. Was my eye gone? Fortunately it was not.

Some time later Skorzeny allowed himself to be treated by his regimental surgeon. He refused any kind of narcotic save alcohol because he wanted to keep a clear head. The surgeon probed with his instruments while Skorzeny gritted his teeth, thinking of the old days when he had been a duelling student in Vienna and had been subjected to the same kind of treatment. But the wound proved clean and the doctor could sew it up, though he was worried about Skorzeny's eye.

Six days later what was left of the 150 Panzer Brigade was relieved and then broken up. The survivors of the jeep teams were collected just outside St Vith and went on to other assignments, again some of them in US disguise. Obersturmbannführer Otto Skorzeny's role in the Battle of the Bulge and in particular 'Operation Grab' was over. But that operation was not finished with him yet.

---

*For some reason M Rupp received a medal from Eisenhower. Years ago, when the author asked him why and for what, he seemed unclear about the reason.

BOOK THREE

End Run

Ende gut, alles gut (All's well that ends well).

Old German saying

The year 1945 opened with another abortive assassination attempt. In the last days of December 1944, Winston Churchill and his Foreign Secretary, Anthony Eden, had flown to Athens in an attempt to resolve the bloody conflict between the two main Greek partisan groups which had begun to fight each other, once the Germans had evacuated the Greek capital. The fighting had become so intense that British paratroopers had been drafted in to tackle the left-wing ELAS guerrillas. Now a major operation was being undertaken to deal with the communist-inspired partisans before Roosevelt, who didn't approve of British interference in Greek affairs, lost patience totally with Churchill, the now junior partner in the 'special relationship'.

On the same day that Skorzeny was so badly wounded, Greek police made a startling discovery, just hours before Churchill was about to convoke a peace conference between the provisional Greek government and the ELAS leaders. In the former German Army HQ in the Greek capital, a hotel which would be the headquarters of the British Party and the Greek government, nearly a ton of dynamite was found in a sewer. It had been placed there just hours after the news had been released that Churchill and Eden were now in the hotel.

The dynamite had been fused, but not lighted. To the surprise of the routine patrol which found the wooden crates in which 1,000 pounds of the high explosive was packed, they bore the name of the German manufacturer. Later it turned out that the explosive was Penthrite, equipped with German electric detonators, a type commonly used by the enemy.

But British sources discounted the suggestion that the assassination attempt had been the work of German agents. Instead, according to the British press release at the time, they 'believed the explosives had been planted by left-wing ELAS forces to destroy the hotel and with it Churchill, Foreign Secretary Eden, Lt Gen. Scobie, British commander in Athens, and Greek Government officials'.

As far as is known, despite the use of a German-made explosive, the Germans were not behind the attempt on Churchill's life, the last of the war. This time the would-be assassins were former allies, whom Churchill

121

had supported with arms and money over the last few years, the Greeks, who were now, in part, busy changing sides.

Naturally Hitler welcomed the breakdown of the Allied coalition. In perhaps his last major speech of the war, on the radio to the nation on 1 January 1945, he ranted:

> I repeat my prophecy of former days: not only will Great Britain be incapable of taming Bolshevism, her own development must necessarily be that of a body infected more and more by this wasting disease.

Unknown to the Führer, who boasted in that midnight speech, 'we fight, no matter where until victory', and warned 'whoever stabs us in the back will die an ignominious death', it was Germany now that possessed 'a body infected more and more by a wasting disease'. For now, it seemed, virtually all his 'paladins', as Hitler often called his top people, were turning against him trying to make a separate peace with the enemy, and, if necessary, assassinate the Leader if he got in the way of that attempt.

Himmler, 'the loyal Heinrich' as Hitler called him, was already negotiating with both the Americans and the Russians – Churchill refused to have any truck with the man who had ordered the kidnapping of Payne and Best. In Berne, his SS generals were trying to work out a surrender deal with Allen Dulles, head of the OSS station. If they could convince the Americans, they reasoned, to agree to an armistice with the German 10th Army in Italy, the rest of the Wehrmacht would go along with it.

Time and time again, Schellenberg tried to convince Himmler, who still believed there would be a role for him in a beaten post-war Germany, that the real obstacle to any negotiated peace was the Führer. Himmler, living off his nerves and worried about saving his own skin, admitted that there were only two remedies left if something was to be saved from the wreckage of the Third Reich – remove the Führer or shoot him. 'But,' as he moaned to the cunning ex-lawyer Schellenberg, 'if I said that to the Führer, he would fly into a violent rage and shoot me out of hand.'

'That's just what you must protect yourself against. You still have enough higher SS leaders and you are still in a strong enough position to arrest him. If there is no other way the doctors will have to intervene.' We don't know whether Schellenberg meant by that remark that Hitler's doctors should certify him insane and incapable of ruling, or that the doctors should take more direct action: have Hitler poisoned.*

---

*I have been told that when the US authorities discovered Dr Morell, the most notorious of the Führer's doctors, in the Bavarian border hamlet of Bayrisch-Gmain after the war, he was trembling all over and moaning that someone was out to kill him. Presumably he meant loyal Hitler followers.

Albert Speer, who unlike Himmler would survive the war, knew by that spring that only the most drastic solution could save something of a ruined Germany. In hospital to which he had been sent suffering from some vague but serious illness and where he had feared for his life, he had continued to do his utmost for the German cause. But when that early spring, Hitler ordered 'Operation Nero', a decree ordering the destruction of anything of importance in the path of the advancing Allies, something which would ruin Germany totally, a scorched earth policy of the kind the Russians had employed back in 1941, he rebelled. There was only one way to stop the rot – kill Hitler. But how?

But before he committed himself to the most drastic course, Speer being Speer, the born survivor, wrote a memorandum on 18 March, in which he stated:

> There is no question but that the German economy will collapse in four to eight weeks. After the collapse the war cannot be continued even militarily. [He went on to tell the Führer that] we have no fight at this stage of the war to carry out demolitions which might affect the very existence of the people . . . On us rests the duty of leaving to the nation every possibility of ensuring its reconstruction in the future.

The memo served only to enrage Hitler, who knew he was defeated, even more. He summoned Speer and cried heatedly:

> If the war is lost, the Reich will also perish! That is inevitable. It is not necessary to worry about the basic requirements for people to continue a primitive existence. On the contrary, it will be better to destroy these things ourselves because this country will have proved to be the weaker one and the future will belong solely to the stronger eastern nation [Hitler meant Russia]. Besides, those who remain after battle will be the inferior ones, for the good ones will have been killed.

According to Speer's own account, that outburst by Hitler finally decided him that he must murder the Führer and save what was left of Germany before it was too late. He knew it had to be a one-man action and he knew, too, that he hadn't the courage or the means of going up to Hitler and shooting him in cold blood, as some of the military plotters on the Führer's life the previous year had suggested the assassination should be carried out.

In the end Speer decided the best plan would be for him to pump poison down the air conditioning chutes of Hitler's bunker and kill him that way. It was to be a strange kind of impersonal assassination and reminiscent of the gas ovens of the concentration camps from which Speer tried to distance himself in post-war years. Naturally Speer, being Speer, never carried the plan out – if there had even been such a plan.*

He would survive to make yet another successful career in post-war Germany and die in the arms of an English lady during a love tryst in a London hotel.

So Hitler headed for his own *Götterdämmerung*. Many top-ranking Germans wanted him assassinated. But that didn't seem to worry the now paranoid Führer. He knew that virtually every one of his former comrades, who thanks to him had risen to the highest posts in the Third Reich, had betrayed him and were actively dealing with the enemy, presumably to save their own skins. It didn't seem to worry him any more. He simply hung on to what was left of his life.

On 22 April 1945 Hitler was visited in Berlin by what his British MI5 interrogators called 'an unrepentant Nazi', General of the SS, Gottlieb Berger. The one time 'Duke of Swabia', as he had been nicknamed, had played a major role in the formation of the SS and its battle tactics. Immediately after his capture, Berger was asked by his British interrogators what he thought had been the manner of Hitler's death. The big Swabian answered:

> I presume that he blew himself up, but he was just as likely to have had a stroke, as he raved like a madman ... He was completely finished, a broken man.

Berger explained that Himmler had tried to convince Hitler to leave Berlin and escape to safety with his, Himmler's, help. That may well have been a play on Himmler's part. Perhaps he had something else planned for the crazy leader. For the 'Loyal Heinrich', just like Speer, Goering, Bormann and the rest, were trying to distance themselves from Hitler and the evil deeds of the Third Reich in the hope that there would be a suitable place for them in a post-war Germany.

Berger maintained: 'I told him [Hitler] that it was out of the question and that he could not betray the German people'.

Hitler was no longer concerned with the German people and their fate. He was completely wrapped up in himself. Hitler raved, according to Berger, 'Everyone has deceived me. The armed forces have lied to me. Finally the SS has left me in the lurch.'

Berger left, escaped from Berlin and then served six and a half years in jail for his wartime role in the SS. He would die peacefully in bed. Hitler, still in Berlin, wouldn't.

*Speer maintained he wrote his famous memoirs while serving his twenty-year sentence for war crimes in Spandau jail. There, however, all his writings were systematically destroyed every thirty days. One wonders where he really wrote them.

Six days after that last meeting with Berger, fifteen heavily armed Italian partisans, under the command of a 'Colonel' (self-styled) Valerio who had fought in the Spanish Civil War, set off to bring the former Duce from the northern Italian township of Dongo where he was under arrest. It was here that Mussolini and his silly but pretty young mistress, Clara Petacci, would meet their end. The post-war official version of that episode was that the partisans had orders to bring the ex-dictator back to Milan. But when Mussolini and his mistress did reach Milan they were already dead.

According to the official story, the partisans reached the house where the two captives were being held. Without ceremony they burst in. 'I have come to rescue you, 'Valerio yelled.

'Really,' was Mussolini's sole reply.

Clara, lying partially unclothed on the bed, started to look for her clothes. Valerio snapped, 'What are you looking for?'

With tears in her eyes, she replied, 'My knickers.' For she had sent Skorzeny's man, Obersturmführer Franz Spoegler, who had been in charge of the two fugitives and the precious valise which contained top secret documents, back to her original home to fetch more clean clothes.*

Valerio said knickers didn't matter. Nor did they. Soon the dead woman would be subjected to nasty sexual abuse, which would have been carried out whether Clara Petacci had worn knickers or not.

Now they were hurried out into the waiting car. With two heavily armed partisans on the running board and two curious fishermen running after the vehicle, the old car ground its way up the steep hill towards the village of Azzano. But it had only gone a few hundred metres when it stopped outside the iron gate of a large shuttered villa.

Valerio dropped over the side. Crouched low as if he expected danger, he checked the villa; then coming back, he cried in a loud voice: 'By the order of the general headquarters of the Volunteers for Freedom Corps, I am required to render justice to the Italian people.'

Clara knew what that meant. She flung herself forward, arms extended protectively, in front of Mussolini: 'No,' she screamed. 'He mustn't die.'

'Move away if you don't want to die, too!' Valerio yelled.

Clara moved to the right. The Duce said nothing. Valerio aimed at Mussolini's chest. He pressed the trigger of his machine pistol. Nothing! He had a stoppage. He pulled out his pistol and tried again. Once more – nothing! It seemed as if Fate didn't want Mussolini to die. He called to one of the partisans, 'Give me your pistol.'

This time Fate looked the other way. At a distance of three metres so that he couldn't miss, Valerio pumped a full magazine into the Duce's one-time barrel chest, now shrunken and deflated. He pitched forward,

---

*Skorzeny had retained an interest in the man he had once rescued and had provided an SS bodyguard for the Duce in his hour of need, a fugitive once more.

dead before he hit the ground. A moment later the former Spanish War veteran turned his weapon on Clara.

Early next morning, their bodies were found slumped, blood-stained and cold, outside a garage not far from the centre of Milan. The mob soon learned who they were. Screaming with rage and overcome by a strange kind of atavistic blood lust, the men and women, even children, went to work on the now hated dictator and his pretty young mistress. As a typical Italian sign of infinite contempt, the men urinated on Mussolini's corpse and then began beating it with sticks, pushing and jostling each other in order to launch vicious kicks at his dead face.

The ultimate indignity was inflicted on Clara. Old crones squatted over her battered face and urinated into her gaping mouth. Twenty-three years earlier Mussolini, armed with little more than an idea, which had inspired Hitler to do the same, had seized power. Now his 'New Romans', as he had called his Italian subjects proudly, had not only murdered him, they were pissing on him too!

Back on 29 July 1943, in an operation that remained a German secret until the end of the war, the Research Institute of the German Post Office managed to tap the underground cable beneath the Atlantic, which linked Britain and America. Not only that, but the scientists of the Reichspost also succeeded in unscrambling the phones used by the Top Brass on both sides of the 'big pond', in particular those of Churchill and Roosevelt, the two partners in Churchill's so-called 'special relationship'.

It was a major technical breakthrough for the German eavesdroppers. Now they could listen to the enemy leaders talking about secret affairs of state. On that July day, the German operatives, glued to their earphones, listened to a conversation, distorted a little by the crackle of static, and heard something of major significance. It was all connected with Italy, the fellow Axis power, which was now secretly discussing an armistice with the Western Allies who had landed in Sicily earlier that month.

The listeners heard Churchill say to Roosevelt: 'We don't want proposals for an armistice to be made before we have definitely been approached.'

'That's right,' Roosevelt agreed.

Then the two Allied leaders talked about the fate of the now missing Duce, Mussolini. Each agreed that the former Italian dictator would end up 'on a hangman's rope'. But how? Churchill was in favour of a 'show trial', which would be 'a healthy lesson for the Nazis', in particular Hitler. Roosevelt was against such a trial. Roosevelt, like most US Presidents before and after him (primarily concerned with 'domestic politics'), thought a legal process against Mussolini might affect the coming presidential elections when he intended to run for a third term. Suddenly the US President urged, 'Couldn't he [Mussolini] die suddenly?' He made the point that several people whom Churchill had regarded as enemies during the war had died 'abruptly' in supposed accidents and the like.

Roosevelt went on to say:

> I think that if Mussolini died while he was still in Italian hands, we would be best served. If we can agree to get rid of him while he is still in their hands ... there'd be no doubt who had killed him. That would upset my Italian voters here in the States.

Churchill still wasn't convinced. He said: 'I can't believe that the votes of a handful of Italian voters in your country can influence your decision.'

Roosevelt pulled no punches; he never did when it came to his success or lack of it at the hustings.

> If I'm not nominated then I won't be elected ... If I lose, our alliance might break up. Stalin will make a separate peace with Germany. Then Hitler will turn his full anger on Britain and, without help, what can you do?

Churchill seemingly remained undecided.

In itself that overheard conversation of 1943 is of only fleeting interest. What is of importance is Roosevelt's belief – and naturally that of other powerful people elsewhere – that Churchill wouldn't hesitate to use even murder to get rid of people who stood in the way of his policies. The mysterious murder of French Admiral Darlan and the speedy dispatch of his French murderers in North Africa in 1942 were cited by Churchill's enemies as an example of the way in which his political opponents were dealt with; or the still unexplained crash of Polish General Sikorski at Gibraltar who stood in Churchill's way during his dealings with Britain's new ally, Soviet Russia.

In the light of what other powerful people, including the US President, thought of Churchill's ruthlessness which wouldn't even stop at political assassination, was the British Prime Minister behind the assassination of the former Italian dictator?

For years now there have been persistent claims in Italy that Mussolini wasn't killed by an Italian at all. The Italian revisionists maintain that the last major assassination of World War Two had already been carried out *before* the partisans arrived. One popular historian, Franco Bandini* states that the former Duce and his mistress were killed by an assassination

---

*Professor de Felice of the University of Rome first made the claim in 1995 in his book *La Guerra Civile*. Since then the Professor's claims have been taken up and amplified by other historians. Even as the author writes, the Italian state radio and television station, RIAS, is preparing a programme on this issue.

squad led by an Englishman, Captain Malcolm Smith. Smith, now dead, was born in Sicily, the son of a British businessman. Some years before the war, because he spoke fluent Italian, he was recruited into the SIS and for that same reason he was employed by the British Secret Service in Italy in 1945.

According to the memoirs of another partisan,* who disappeared mysteriously two years after the assassination this is what happened: 'They [Smith and three gunmen under his command] entered the room where Mussolini and Clara were held. They led them out about 10 p.m. A short time later shots were heard.'

As Lonati, one of the killers, told it:

> The Englishman told me that we would have to shoot them and it would have to be one of us Italians to fire. We went out of the house and after following the path for two hundred metres, I fired several machine-gun shots without aiming at the heart of Il Duce. Almost simultaneously 'John' [Smith's *nom de guerre*] opened fire on the woman. It was just after 11 p.m. on 28 April 1945.

Thereafter, according to revisionist historians in Italy, a second 'execution' was carried out by the communist partisans under 'Valerio' (real name Walter Audisio). We don't know if Valerio was present when the only verified contact between an undercover British agent and the Italian communist partisans took place in Milan. The agent, Massimo Salvadori, an SOE agent with the partisans, told the Partisan Council that when Mussolini was found, and he would undoubtedly be captured soon, he should be killed to avoid 'unwelcome' publicity which would attend any attempt to put the ex-Duce on trial.

Now, as the revisionists see it, Valerio was faced with a dilemma. Should he report to the Council that he had failed? Mussolini was already dead. Or should he report that he and the other communist partisans had done the deed themselves? After all that would be a tremendous propaganda coup for the communists who at that time were attempting to take over Northern Italy. *They* were the ones who had dealt with the class enemy Mussolini.**

But whether Churchill had been party to the assassination of Mussolini or not, it is clear that in that last week of the war, he must have given his

---

*Franco Magni: *Rebels of the Resistance in Pre-Alpine Lombardy*.
**The existence of SOE agent Salvadori has been backed up by the son of another SOE operative, Capt. Richard Cooper. When he returned from the war, he showed his son, soon to be an officer in the SAS, a black tassel cap of the type worn by Mussolini and other high-ranking fascists. His son asked him if it was the Duce's. He wouldn't answer. As his son remembers, 'He was always happy to talk about other things'.

approval to finally do away with the other remaining dictator, Hitler. The truce of 1939/40 had long disappeared in the maelstrom of total warfare. Now, as throughout Europe political opponents in both enemy and allied countries were being 'liquidated' (in de Gaulle's France it was reported that up to 100,000 *collabos* and dangerous political opponents were dealt with between 1944 and 1945), Churchill must have sanctioned 'Bomber' Harris's plan to deal with the Führer once and for all.

Back in the summer of 1943, Harris had sworn that Berlin would be hammered 'until the heart of Nazi Germany would cease to exist'. Hard man that he was – Harris had once been stopped by a young policeman and told if he continued to speed in his big American car, he'd kill someone. Coldly, 'Bomber' had replied, 'young man I kill hundreds every night' – he now ordered that Hitler should be dealt with at last in his own home. The Führer had escaped, so Allied Intelligence reasoned, from his ruined capital Berlin. So where could he be? The answer was obvious. 'Wolf', the alias Hitler had used before he achieved power in '33, had returned to his mountain lair.

In that last week of April, Allied Intelligence felt there were only two possible places where Hitler might now be holed up since his East Prussian headquarters had been overrun by the Red Army. Either he was in Berlin, or at his 'Eagle's Nest' in the Bavarian Alps above the township of Berchtesgaden. Due to the fact that reports coming from Switzerland and relayed to Washington and London by Allen Dulles of the OSS, that the Germans were building up a kind of last ditch mountain fortress in the Austrian-German Alps, Allied Intelligence was inclined to think that Hitler had already headed for Berchtesgaden where he could lead the Nazis' fight to the finish.

The bulk of the Reichsbank's gold bullion had already been sent to the area to disappear in perhaps the biggest robbery in history. Goering had gone in the same direction, followed by Foreign Minister von Ribbentrop who had taken up residence in his stolen Austrian castle. More importantly, 'Sepp' Dietrich's beaten 6th SS Panzer Army was retreating from Hungary, followed by the Red Army, heading for Austria and the same general area.

Thus the Allied planners decided if they were finally going to assassinate Hitler, they would find him in his mountain home, built for him over the last decade by Bormann, in which the Nazi *Prominenz*, just like Mafia chieftains, had erected their own homes to be close to Hitler.

Once it had simply been a rural beauty spot, with a couple of modest hotels surrounded by small hill farms that had been in the same hands for centuries. Bormann had changed all that. He had bribed, threatened and blackmailed the *Erbbaueren* (the hereditary farmers, as they were called) to abandon their farms, sold their land at premium rates to fellow Nazis and then, as war loomed, erected a military complex to protect the Führer whenever he was in residence on the 'Mountain' among the 'Mountain People', as the Nazis called the place and themselves.

After he had completed his 50th birthday present for the Führer, the 'Eagle's Nest', which Hitler visited only five times and which cost 30 million marks to construct,* Bormann had turned his attention to making the whole 'mountain' complex as secure as possible, both from the land and the air.

Bormann, 'the Brown Eminence' as he was known, the secretive party secretary, who in reality wielded more power on the German home front than Hitler himself, declared the whole 'Mountain' *sperrgebiet* (off limits). A battalion of the Waffen SS was stationed there permanently. Together with mountain troops from nearby Bad Reichenhall, the SS patrolled the boundaries of this prohibited area twenty-four hours a day, something which the British planners of 'Operation Foxley' had not reckoned with.

Then Bormann turned his attention to the threat of an air attack. Great air raid shelters were dug, not only for the Führer and the *Prominenz*, but also for the guards, servants and foreign workers – there was even a cinema which could hold 8,000 people. Chemical companies were brought in and stationed at strategic points on the mountain. As soon as the first warning of an enemy air attack was given, they could produce a smoke screen, which, in theory, could cover the key parts of the area in a matter of minutes. Finally there were the fighter bases such as Furstenfeldbruck in the Munich area where the Messerschmitts could be scrambled to ward off any aerial attack from the west or indeed over the Alps from the newer Allied air bases in Italy.

Whether it was because of Bormann's precautions, the problem of flying over the Alps in a heavy, bomb-laden aircraft, or Allied scruples about bombing an enemy politician's home, the 'Mountain' had not been seriously troubled by air raids until now. 'Bomber' Harris was determined to end all that. If anyone could, Harris swore, he'd blast Berchtesgaden off the map.

To do so, he picked one of his most experienced bomber commanders. This was 24-year-old Wing-Commander Basil Templeman-Rooke, who had begun his bomber career in 1943. By the end of that year he had already been awarded the DFC and more importantly had flown over the Alps to bomb Turin in the hope that a bombing raid on that city, so far away from England, would encourage the Italians to surrender.

After one tour of ops, Templeman-Rooke commenced another one in May '44. He took part in the pre-D-Day bombing of French railways, storage depots, etc., and then in the attacks on V-1 sites after the Invasion.

*The Tea House (the Americans gave it its 'Eagle's Nest' name) was a gigantic feat of engineering and even today it can only be reached by a special bus from May to October when the road up to the mountain top is clear of snow.

The controversial bombing of Dresden followed in February '45. Shortly thereafter he had been given the command of the RAF's 170 Squadron and awarded a Bar to his DFC and in March, the DSO.

For Harris, the young squadron commander must have seemed the ideal leader for what he had in mind for the 170th Squadron. He was young, brave, very experienced and, above all, lucky. In his two years of combat he had survived over forty missions, and even when he had been hit by flak over Gelsenkirchen, he had brought his Lancaster back on two engines and crash-landed the four-engined plane without injury. Now Harris ordered Templeman-Rooke to fly his squadron's last combat mission of the war, its target perhaps the most important one left in Germany that last April of the war.

For days now, although the hilltops were still covered with snow down to 900 metres causing fog, reconnaissance planes kept flying over the 'mountain', setting off the wail of the sirens and the populace scurrying for the shelters. Then once again the smoke screen would descend on the deserted homes of the *Prominenz*. For even Hitler's most devoted followers had reasoned that the 'mountain' was no place to be at this stage of the war. Still there had as yet been no attempt to bomb the area.

That changed at 09.30 on the morning of Wednesday 25 April 1945. On the half hour precisely, the pre-alarm sirens started to sound. Obediently the locals began to file into their air-raid shelters, believing that as was customary nothing much would happen. This time they were wrong. Most of the 'mountain', right up to the 'Eagle's Nest' at 9,300 feet, was obscured by fog. This time on Harris's order, 170 Squadron, part of a force of 318 Lancasters, was determined to carry out their mission. Within half an hour of the pre-alarm being sounded, the first bombs were raining down on the twin heights of Klaus-and-Buchenhoehe.

Then came the second raid. According to German reports, the Lancasters swept in not much later, dropping 500 lb bombs. Immediately Hitler's Berghof was hit, where back in what now seemed another age, the Führer had once received British PM Chamberlain, the 'Umbrella-Man' as the Germans had mocked him due to his gamp and appearance. Afterwards, as German eye-witnesses recorded, the interior looked like a landscape after an earthquake. Goering's house, demolished together with his swimming pool, followed. Bormann's house received a direct hit.* The only place that was not destroyed or damaged was the 'Eagle's

---

*Even today, at a certain angle, you can see the series of depressions leading up to where Goering's house was, and that mark one bomber's run in to the attack. Of the house itself only a few steps remain next to some bushes where visitors allow their dogs to do their business – 'Hundepissecke' the locals call it. One wonders what roly-poly 'Fat Hermann' (Goering) would have said. Probably he would have reached for his shotgun and started blazing away; he was always very keen to shoot anything in four legs.

Nest'. It had been well camouflaged with tin leaves and was perhaps too small a target for Harris's men. But as the bombers swept on to attack nearby Bad Reichenhall, where 200 people were killed that day, they left behind them only smoking wreckage, which would be added to when the SS guards retreated, setting fire to everything they could not loot.

But the RAF's raid on the 'mountain' had been in vain. Templeman-Rooke had been misinformed. The Führer was not in residence. He had remained in his bunker, spared yet again by the 'providence' in which he believed so strongly. But he knew he couldn't go on for ever. As he declared to anyone prepared still to listen to him in his Berlin bunker, he wasn't going to die at 'the hands of the mob' like his friend and fellow dictator Mussolini. Nor was he going to allow himself to be 'paraded through the streets of Moscow' in a cage. So, a broken man, embittered at the failings of his own people, and perhaps a little mad, the leader who had survived so many assassination attempts, died by his own hand. His 'providence' had run out at last.

Aftermath: Trial and Escape

Plot to slay Ike called hoax. Designed to boost Nazi morale

Headline in *Stars and Stripes*, 22 May 1945

It was perhaps ironic that on the day when Hitler's 'providence' ran out and his vaunted '1,000 Year Reich' collapsed after a mere twelve years, the American OSS had a company of paratroopers ready on the tarmac of their airfield in Italy, prepared to sacrifice their lives, if necessary, to assassinate a fellow countryman. They were volunteers recruited from US POW camps in that country who were going to drop on the 'mountain' and finally deal with their one-time fellow countryman, Adolf Hitler, born in nearby Braunau-am-Inn. They were, of course, Austrians, who now felt themselves 'liberated' by the Amis from the 'Nazi yoke'. But of course they weren't needed. Their 'oppressor' was dead and they would no longer need to risk their lives in an attempt to assassinate him.

On that day, it might have seemed to those who had fought in the brutal, no-holds-barred war in the shadows over the last two years that there was still another fellow Austrian who needed to be brought to book. This was the man whom Eisenhower, the Austrian volunteers' new boss, had once called 'the most dangerous man in Europe', Obersturmbann-führer Otto Skorzeny.

They and the Allied Intelligence Services would not have had to look far for the scarfaced giant. For he had taken up residence in those same Alps, in a hut on the Dachstein Mountain. By then he had released his Belgian and Dutch volunteers from his Jagdkommando and was lazing away his days in an alpine hut with a few select comrades, wondering what to do next, until he learned from peasant contacts in the valley below that the Amis were looking for him.

Skorzeny decided he had better surrender. He sent a letter to the nearest US commander, advising him of his presence on the mountain. There was no answer. Meanwhile Radio Luxembourg, the Allied-controlled broadcasting station which Skorzeny could hear, appealed to its listeners to help find the 'war criminal Skorzeny'. The newspapers took up the hue and cry. And still the Americans below, enjoying the peace, especially the willing 'frowleins' seemed uninterested in their prominent guests on top of the mountain. Another letter went down to the valley. Again no answer.

Finally Skorzeny decided that if the Amis wouldn't come to him, he'd go to them. He went down the mountain with his adjutant, his first general staff officer Captain Hunke, and an interpreter, Lieutenant Peter. There he made arrangements for a jeep to pick him up at a certain bridge. The Amis were not interested. It was taking the man who had rescued Mussolini and probably planned to kill the Supreme Commander time to realise that he was no longer important; he was just another Nazi on the run in the Austro-German Alps and there were thousands of them.

Thus it was that eleven days after the German official surrender, Skorzeny and his three men walked into the American Army HQ in nearby Salzburg in German uniform, fully armed and wearing white bands around their sleeves above the SS insignia.

Still it wasn't easy. The American sergeant to whom the four surrendered had never heard of Otto Skorzeny. But if they felt that important, he told them, he would take them in his jeep to divisional headquarters and they could surrender there – unless they wanted to take off their uniforms and do 'a dive', as it was called.

They didn't. Perhaps Skorzeny had plans for further employment in the kind of clandestine warfare that had been his speciality, even if it meant working for the former enemy. So they set off for divisional HQ, with a GI driver who told them when he heard Skorzeny's name: 'If you're really Skorzeny, you'd better take a drink, 'whereupon he offered the giant a bottle of wine, 'because tonight they'll hang you.' But war criminal or not the Americans had no intention of hanging Skorzeny.

At divisional HQ again no one seemed particularly interested in the four SS men. Finally a US major appeared and told them to go elsewhere to pick up orders. And all this time they were still armed. Then finally someone in the US Third Division ('the Rock of the Marne') realised exactly who they had captured, if that is the right word for it. Skorzeny was asked to enter a requisitioned Austrian villa for an interview with two young American officers. Bewildered but amused, he did as was requested. Hardly had he taken a step inside when all the windows were flung open and tommy guns were thrust through, pointing straight at him.

Now the Amis were no longer casual. He was disarmed and stripped naked. He was given a rapid examination to ascertain if he had an 'L-pill' hidden in his mouth, anus or behind his testicles. The Americans were cutting the vain Jagdkommando leader down to size. Thereafter he was bundled into a jeep. An MP armed with a 'grease-gun' sat next to him, holding his weapon pointed right at Skorzeny's face. Covered by armoured cars, the jeep was driven back to Salzburg where he gave his first interview to the correspondents of the foreign press. The Skorzeny legend was entering a new chapter.

'Skorzeny certainly looks the part,' the female representative of the *New*

York Times wrote. 'He is striking in a rough way: a huge powerful figure. "The Beast of Belsen"* is something out of the nursery in comparison.' Then in her article the next day she added, presumably for the sake of her female readers, 'He has blue eyes.'

A British reporter present wrote:

> It was thought best to keep Skorzeny with his hands manacled behind his back. When he was given a cigarette it was lit and he had to have the ash shaken off. A glass of water was held to his lips.

But despite the descriptive prose about Skorzeny's person, it was clear that the correspondents' first and main interest was the alleged plot to kill General Eisenhower, the Supreme Commander, during the Battle of the Bulge.

Ed Lawrence of the Army's newspaper *Stars and Stripes* headlined his story '*Nazi Who Saved Duce Boasts of Plot to Slay Eisenhower*' He went on to report on 18 May:

> Lt Col. Otto R Skorzeny, scar-faced 6 foot 4 professional Nazi kidnapper and killer today boasted to his Third Div. captors of having master-minded a plot to slay Gen. Eisenhower . . . Disguised in GI uniforms, Skorzeny's men tried to infiltrate American lines early in the Ardennes offensive under pretence of bringing German prisoners to SHAEF for questioning. They hoped to get close enough to Gen. Eisenhower to kill him.

The *New York Times* correspondent made the same point:

> He [Skorzeny] smilingly disclaimed credit for leading a mission to murder members of the Allied High Command last winter . . . if any German soldiers operated behind the American lines in American uniform, it was something that someone else, not he, had cooked up.

Of course Skorzeny had not led a group of Germans dressed as GIs personally. But the commando leader did not deny that there might have been a plan to assassinate Eisenhower, which he might have taken part in, if necessary. As he told the assembled correspondents:

> *If* I had ever been ordered to attack GHQ [he was careful not to mention Eisenhower by name], I should have made a plan to do so. If I had made a plan, I would have carried it out. And no one would have been left in doubt about what I was trying to do.

*The ugly commandant of Belsen Concentration Camp.

Now in American captivity with a charge of being a potential war criminal hanging over his big head – soon Allied countries from Belgium to Russia would be asking for his extradition – Skorzeny was letting his habitual vanity run away with him. Perhaps he guessed he was in some danger, but he took all Americans to be as naive as the war correspondents, who obviously admired him. He felt that he could afford to boast about his exploits, even the plot to kill Eisenhower. After all the Americans were hanging on his every word, weren't they?

In a report filed that same day and originating from the headquarters of the Seventh US Army to which the 3rd Infantry Division belonged, the headline proclaimed quite unequivocally: 'Plot Against Eisenhower Failed'.*

The report on what Skorzeny had done differed in detail from the other reports. It stated: 'Skorzeny and his accomplices ... dressed as British officers. His mission was to make his way to Allied headquarters, then in Paris, and assassinate General Eisenhower.' But whatever the alleged method Skorzeny was supposed to have used in his men's attempt to kill Eisenhower, there was no doubt that the American authorities believed, as they had done in the dark December of 1944, that the attempt had been made. After all the final report didn't come from the admiring US press corps, but from the headquarters of a large US army, the Seventh.

It can be conjectured that whoever allowed that report to be released at Seventh Army HQ that May day came in for a great deal of sorrow. For the unknown press officer undoubtedly set the cat among the pigeons at Supreme Headquarters.

On that very same day, Skorzeny, who according to his account, had experienced so much difficulty surrendering to the Amis, was confronted with 'one of the most decent and fairest of all my interrogators' as Skorzeny described him. He always believed that this US colonel, who interrogated him at Augsburg, Germany to which he had been hurriedly taken from Salzburg, was the Seventh Army's head of counterintelligence. He wasn't. He was that same Lt Colonel Gordon Sheen, who had burst into Strong's office that grim December day crying, 'Skorzeny is driving on Paris.'

For six long hours Sheen grilled the big Austrian. He told the latter of all the rumours that had circulated at that time. He made Skorzeny laugh with his account of the French pharmacist who had called the CIC from Toul and reported that Skorzeny had been into his shop and bought a packet of aspirins for a headache before continuing his drive on Paris. Naturally Sheen put words into Skorzeny's mouth. He explained that the 'Eisenhower assassination attempt' had just been 'one hell of a rumour'.

New York Times, 18 May 1945.

Equally naturally, Skorzeny, who may well have now begun to realise that his life might be at stake, especially if the Americans handed him over to the Russians, started to agree that they were rumours caused probably by 'Leutnant N' (if he already dreamed up that mysterious officer by then).

On 22 May Sheen gave an exclusive interview to the *Stars and Stripes*. Under the headline, 'Plot to Slay Ike Called Hoax, Designed to Boost Nazi Morale', Sheen was reported to have said in Paris:

> The Nazi super plot to assassinate Gen. Eisenhower was a hoax. The plot was devised within the German Army to boost the morale of the Nazi spies and saboteurs who were to create confusion behind Allied lines during the German counter-offensive last December but the Germans never intended to carry it out.
>
> Sheen said that although precautions were doubled in the case of high-ranking Allied officers, there was no evidence that any attempt against them was contemplated.

Why had Sheen changed his attitude to the supposed assassination so radically when only six months earlier he had upset the routine of Allied Supreme Headquarters so much that Eisenhower and most of his senior staff had virtually become prisoners for the crucial first ten days of America's greatest land battle of the 20th century? Why, too, had Sheen rushed to interview Skorzeny at Augsburg using a false identity? Why were his questions in the form that he relayed them to the press and PR men always phrased in a way that related to an attack on Supreme or Allied Headquarters and never on that HQ's Supreme Commander, General Eisenhower himself? And finally, why on 11 July 1945, two months after Sheen had dismissed the assassination story as a hoax, did the US 12th Army Group file the following charge against Skorzeny: 'Offense, Wearing US uniforms obtained from Red Cross packages. Plan for the assassination of Gen. EISENHOWER'?

On 18 August 1947 Skorzeny and ten of his former commandos went on trial at Dachau outside Munich before a US General Military Court.

His trial was regarded as a 'secondary proceeding', not to be compared with the trial of the major German war criminals at the International Military Tribunal in Nuremberg. These 'secondary proceedings' had been going on in the grounds of Germany's most infamous concentration camp since 15 November 1945 with most of the accused being military. They included the notorious 'Malmedy Massacre Case' in which former SS General Sepp Dietrich and SS Colonel Peiper were the main accused. Soon it would be Skorzeny's time to stand trial before what was regarded by the Germans as a prejudiced court.

For these court proceedings at the 'Dachau Trials', as they were popularly known, were not conducted like a typical trial under the American judicial system. Guilt was established *beforehand* by tough interrogators assigned to obtain confessions from the accused who were then assumed guilty, with the burden of proof being placed on the defence.

All the personnel involved, prosecution, defence and jury, were US military officers. In the case of the judge (or judges) they took notice of the crimes allegedly committed, which meant that the defence was not permitted to argue that the crimes had not taken place. Hearsay testimony was permitted, as were affidavits submitted by witnesses who didn't need to attend the count. That meant these witnesses could not be cross-examined by the defence. Indeed the proceedings were so framed that even some of the accused were not permitted to testify in their own defence.

The accused had one additional legal hurdle to overcome. It was, as the 'Jewish Virtual Library' frankly admits, the fact that:

> The American prosecutors in the Dachau proceedings, most of whom were Jewish, had only to walk a few yards to the infamous gas chamber . . . to know what the Germans were capable of. The use of these former German Jews as interrogators, prosecution lawyers and judges was not a deliberate provocation on the part of the US authorities, it was simply a matter of necessity.

The Americans needed, as the 'Jewish Virtual Library' puts it, 'all the help they could get from native German speakers, which is the reason that German-Jewish refugees were used in the investigative process'.*

The charges against Skorzeny and the other accused were read out by Colonel Rosenfeld, a Jewish American lawyer, who had worked in Field Security during the Battle of the Bulge and since the war had been functioning as judge or legal officer in most of the 'Dachau Trials'. Rosenfeld, a sharp-faced, bespectacled officer, looked as if he would stand no nonsense from the 'Nazis' and during the proceedings, which would last into September 1947, that was proved to be true.

Since Skorzeny's first arraignment in 1945, the charges against him had changed somewhat. They now read, in the long-winded language of the US legal profession:

> Skorzeny . . . and divers other persons, German nationals or persons acting with German nationals, at sundry times between 10 Dec 1944 and about 15 January 1945 . . . acting in a common design to commit the acts hereinafter alleged, did wrongly encourage, aid, abet and

*See: C Whiting, *Massacre at Malmedy* for further details.

participate in the killing, shooting, ill-treatment, abuse and torture of members of the Armed Forces of the United States of America, who were then and there surrendered and unarmed prisoners of war in the custody of the then German Reich, the exact names and numbers of such persons being unknown but aggregating over one hundred.

It was a blanket charge, based on a shaky foundation, that some sort of mass murder and massacre had taken place on unknown US soldiers. It couldn't and wouldn't stand up in court. In essence, however, there was something that could be proven. It was as Rosenfeld read it out, that the malefactors had also participated in

removing, appropriating and using uniforms, identification documents, insignia of rank, decorations and other effects and objects of personal use in the possession of members of the Armed Forces of the United States of America . . .

Added to that was 'the use and benefit [by the accused] in obstructing and preventing the receipt and delivery of Red Cross and other parcels, containing food and clothing consigned to members of the Armed Forces of the United States.'

In brief then, Skorzeny, the man who had rescued Mussolini, kidnapped Horthy's son, had Eisenhower imprisoned in his own HQ for nearly two weeks, etc. was now being accused of stealing uniforms for his commandos and making use of the Swiss Red Cross parcels intended for US POWs!

Up to now, Skorzeny, still wanted, as we have seen, in half a dozen countries, had been regarded as a fairly important war criminal. Now he was being tried at Dachau for what was essentially a trivial misdemeanour. Soldiers of all times and nations had looted and stolen throughout the ages; it didn't make them war criminals.

Durst, who was Jewish and Skorzeny's defending lawyer, gave the ex-commando leader an exceedingly hard time. Later Skorzeny admitted that it was the toughest grilling he had ever experienced. After four days in court, Skorzeny was in his cell when Durst walked in, shook him by the hand for the first time and smiled: 'I am sure of your innocence on every charge. Now I know you have nothing to hide, I shall fight for you as if you were my brother.'

Skorzeny had been warned by German lawyers for the defence not to trust the American advocate. He ignored their advice. He put his full trust in the American and he was rewarded for that trust.

In the last week of August Skorzeny took the stand himself to explain his actions during the Battle of the Bulge. He didn't deny that he and his men actually wore American uniforms during the course of operations.

His defence was that he had not been alone in doing this. Virtually every other Allied nation had used the same trick, including the Americans themselves during their attack on the German city of Aachen.

It was during the course of this Skorzeny marathon that Colonel Durst did something unexpected and very usual. He asked Skorzeny during a routine questioning of one of his commandos, 'Now, you and your men were the same ones that talked about the capture of Eisenhower, weren't you?'

The prosecutor Colonel Rosenfeld jumped in immediately. He snapped, 'If the court please, Prosecution objects to this, as not being cross-examination.'

The law member turned to Durst and said, 'Counsel?'

Durst said, 'It certainly is cross examination because I want to show that this man discussed and told some of the wildest rumours that have ever been around here and that this is one of them he specifically discussed.'

The president stepped in immediately and said, 'Subject to the objection of any member of the court the objection of the Prosecution is overruled.'

But Durst was not going to shut up. A minute or so later, he raised the Eisenhower matter again, this time calling 'Ike' by his present rank, 'Chief of Staff'.*

> I object to this, if it please the court, it is not cross-examination and there is nothing within the four corners of this bill of particulars which has anything to do with the Chief of Staff.

And that was that. Durst was overruled again and the question was struck off the record. Thus the plot against Eisenhower was not raised again and the accusation which had been levelled against Skorzeny, after Sheen had said there had been no plot and the supposed assassination attempt was a 'hoax', was left open.

Now Durst, who raised the apparently taboo Eisenhower Plot question, went on to show that Skorzeny had engaged in a new kind of warfare, more in keeping with the age of strategic bombing and nuclear weapons, and, of course, irregular warfare. To back up his case, Durst called a very surprising witness.

He was Wing Commander Yeo-Thomas, the legendary 'white rabbit', who had worked as an undercover agent with the French Resistance, had been captured, sent to Buchenwald and left a corpse behind to cover his escape. Immediately after the war he had given evidence at the Buchenwald war crimes trial, which had resulted in twenty-two of his guards being sentenced to death.

Now he gave evidence for a man he must have once regarded as a

---

*By then Eisenhower was in Washington acting as the US Army's senior officer.

deadly enemy. He explained how he had used a German uniform to rescue a fellow resistance worker.

Durst asked, 'Did you obtain German uniforms for this purpose?'

Yeo-Thomas said he did.

'How were they obtained?' Durst asked.

'The details I could not tell you. I gave instructions to obtain uniforms by hook or by crook.' The little man in RAF uniform had made his meaning clear enough. The uniforms might have been obtained by murder.

A few moments later he was even clearer.

'To prevent danger of discovery, what would the practice be?'

Yeo-Thomas didn't hesitate. He said softly, 'Bump off the other guy.'

The prosecution had lost its case. As Yeo-Thomas came from the witness stand, Skorzeny and the others stood silently to attention. Later when Skorzeny sent Yeo-Thomas a note of thanks, Yeo-Thomas who was now a director of the Parisian dressmaker Molyneux, replied: 'You did a damned good war job. I'm sure you'll get off. In any case I have a flat in Paris, if you should need somewhere to lie up.'

Later when Skorzeny was transferred, cleared of guilt, to an internment camp, he wrote to the little man for advice on what to do next. The latter's advice was to the point and laconic. It was 'escape!'.

Skorzeny duly did escape. Easily. Much too easily some people thought. Skorzeny had long maintained he would take the greatest pleasure in confronting a German De-Nazification Tribunal and laying his cards – all of them – on the table. Not only would the German court hear all about the turncoats, the one-time Nazis, who were now becoming big shots in the new and emerging German government, but he'd relate what he knew of the Amis and their particular secrets. And the Amis wouldn't like that one bit, especially as he knew of the current deal between the emerging CIA (based on the OSS) and the one-time Nazi spymaster in the east, General Gehlen.*

On 27 July 1948 three ex-SS officers in civilian clothes, driving a car supplied by Skorzeny's new American friends, made a long journey from Hannover in the north of Germany to Wurzburg in the south, not far from the camp where Skorzeny was interned. Here the three stopped to change into US uniforms, replace their car plates with those of the US Army of Occupation, and continued their journey to the Wurzburg camp as 'white mice', i.e. American military policemen.

At the camp the three bogus MPs entered the guard room and stated

---

*The Gehlen Organization, as it was called, would supply the new CIA with perhaps eighty per cent of the information the latter sought on the Russians – and incidentally help to create the 'Cold War'.

briskly: 'We're here to take the Prisoner Skorzeny to Nuremberg for his hearing scheduled for tomorrow.' The guard commander didn't suspect the three SS officers, although their accents must have sounded very foreign. Perhaps in light of what happened, he had been ordered not to ask too many questions. He released the 'Prisoner Skorzeny' without hesitation.

And with that they were gone, together with the scarfaced giant. With a little help from the Gehlen Organization and their American bosses, the Amis had got rid of the boastful, vain ex-commando leader for a while. For Skorzeny knew too many secrets. He knew where the bodies were buried, especially those connected with the plot, real or imagined, to assassinate the Supreme Commander, General Eisenhower that dark December.

Eisenhower: The Captive Hero

'In the strongest possible language you can command, you may say that I have no political ambitions at all.'

General Eisenhower to reporters, Abilene, 1945

Back in that terrible week of December 1944, when Eisenhower's PR man Commander Butcher had remarked, 'Now you know how it must feel to be President and always under the watchful eye of the Secret Service', he probably wanted to cheer up his glum boss. But there was quite a bit of truth in his off-the-cuff remark. It was supported by General Patton, who had grown to dislike his old comrade greatly. 'Ole Blood an' Guts' was already predicting in 44/45 that the Supreme Commander was already preparing his way to become a future President. When in March Eisenhower visited 3rd Army HQ and praised Patton's men, one of the latter's aides remarked he had never done that before. Scornfully the 3rd Army Commander snapped back: 'My Third Army represents an awful lot of votes.'

It wasn't unusual for successful US army commanders to become President. After all several of them, from Washington to Grant, had been elected to that high office. Indeed Patton himself had been asked in April 1945 whether he would become the leader of America's conservatives, the Republicans. He had refused.

Eisenhower himself advanced all sorts of cogent reasons why a man like himself, who had spent all his life in the military, was not suitable for the office of President. As he stated to the reporters in 1945 when he arrived at a homecoming celebration in his honour at Abilene:

> In the strongest language you can command you may say that I have no political ambitions. Make it even stronger than that if you can. I'd like to go further than Sherman in expressing myself on that subject.

Sherman had said, when offered a chance to run for the presidency, that if nominated he would not run, if elected he would not serve. But Eisenhower never would go that far. But still in the early years he spent in Washington as the chief-of-staff of the US Army before he finally 'retired',* he was constantly barraged with offers to run, from first the

*The retirement didn't last long. After being President of Columbia University for a while he 'joined' the army to command NATO.

Democrats and then the Republicans. For he was to these would-be 'kingmakers', which included Richard Nixon and Foster Allen Dulles, brother of the wartime OSS spymaster, the 'captive hero'. He did not need to know anything about politics. All he needed to do was to look the hero and they would look after the rest.

But 'Ike' was not universally liked and admired throughout the USA. The kingmakers were discovering that he might have feet of clay. The British had not, after all, thought much of him as a military leader. As Sir Ian Jacob, the British military secretary to the War Cabinet, noted about his HQ: '[There is] a general air of restless confusion with everyone doing his best under unnatural conditions.'

General MacArthur, his one-time boss in the Far East, also joined in the criticism of the 'captive hero', especially in regard to his conduct of the Battle of the Bulge. MacArthur and his cronies maintained that Marshall sent 'Ike' a stinging reprimand at that time that would have forced any other general to resign.

Earlier Eisenhower himself had been worried about the way that battle would go down with the public. In December 1945 he wrote to Secretary of War Pattison:

> I have been informed that many of the Army's sincere friends are considerably disturbed by certain implications and insinuations . . . in the press concerning the so-called Battle of the Bulge.

Eisenhower went on to state that, in his opinion, the Department of War should not undertake any account of the battle in print. Such a thing might hurt the honour and prestige of the US Army. And his own naturally. For Eisenhower knew that in years to come, he would not be seen merely as the general who had won America's greatest victory in Europe, he would also be subjected to the scrutiny of a wider public, some of whom would undoubtedly be hostile to him. Eisenhower, aiming to become President, might well be regarded differently from 'Ike', the great democratic soldier. His record would be thoroughly checked. His strengths and weaknesses would be rigorously examined.

So what would the Great American Public make of the fact that their potential President had spent the first crucial days of the Bulge secreted away in his HQ, his own role being taken by a double, who possibly risked his life daily as he went to work dressed as a four-star general? While Hodges and Bradley, his two senior generals, played no active part in the battle and the great majority of American troops were secretly placed under the command of an Englishman, Montgomery,* he hid in Versailles. What would they think of that, when 80,000 GIs

*See: C Whiting, *The Field Marshal's Revenge.*

were destined to die, be wounded or captured before it was all over?

It would be understandable, therefore, if all traces of what really happened at Versailles after Sheen had come running into General Strong's office, crying his warning about Skorzeny, should be removed before it became common knowledge.

Colonel Baldwin, who had doubled for the Supreme Commander, disappeared to the front to command an obscure infantry regiment. As a still serving officer he was unable to give his account of the experience. Strong kept quiet for nearly thirty years until he discovered what had happened behind his back.

As he wrote to this author: 'It was twenty-five years before I found out that Bedell Smith had launched a secret inquiry into pre-Bulge intelligence'. Strong was even more surprised to discover that by 'some mistake or other' both copies of the top secret intelligence summaries for that critical week had 'been shredded or burnt by some strange oversight'. We don't need a crystal ball to know who arranged for that. Thereafter, he briefly mentioned the assassination plot in his book *Intelligence at the Top*.

General Bedell Smith, who had virtually run Supreme HQ during the ten days of the 'great flap', had reasons of his own for keeping mum about that period. In the months immediately after the war, he was involved in those very secret and sensitive negotiations with the Gehlen Organization, which would lead to top-level co-operation between the two recent deadly enemies and the founding of the CIA.

What would the Great American Public make of an American general, already dealing with a German one in Washington, who had been one of Hitler's top intelligence experts and a close associate of the alleged killer, Skorzeny? After all the two, Gehlen and Skorzeny, had worked together closely in Russia during the war. Why, Gehlen may well have known of the assassination plot. If it had actually existed. There remained only Skorzeny. How could those who were eager to protect the 'captive hero's' reputation silence the vain, talkative Austrian?

On 10 May 1945, two days after the end of the war, the Joint Chiefs of Staff ordered a victorious Eisenhower to arrest all suspected war criminals. However, the Top Brass advised the Supreme Commander, 'to make some exceptions as you deem advisable for intelligence and other military reasons'. Thus it must have been something of a shock when Skorzeny, whom they had probably thought dead or fled to South America, came down from the Dachstein mountain and virtually asked to be arrested. Perhaps that's why no one wanted to apprehend him at first; Eisenhower would have preferred the Austrian to have gone away. But Skorzeny was connected with the alleged Eisenhower assassination plot and was also a war criminal, whose name and deeds were known to the world and, in addition, was wanted by half a dozen Allied countries in both east and west.

Thus it was that the US authorities had no alternative but to arrest Skorzeny, and despite Sheen's denial that there had been a plot to kill the Supreme Commander, accuse Skorzeny of plotting to kill him.

Fortunately for the would-be 'kingmakers' however, the whole business of the war crime trials was almost totally in the hands of the Americans. In the US Zone of Occupation, where most of the major trials took place, there were 2,000 Americans involved to only 170 British. The Americans dominated the administration, transport, feeding, overall security, etc. in the three years after the war in which the proceedings took place. In essence they could defer trials, dominate both prosecution and defence, and change the original charges as they wished, without seeking agreement from their former allies.

In August 1945, for instance, a Colonel Dando of the US Counter-Intelligence Branch was asked by two Danish officers whether they could question Skorzeny on his activities with the Gestapo in wartime Denmark. The Colonel refused. The two officers then said, 'they had been told that SKORZENY would soon go to England.' Dando replied, 'there was not the slightest question of SKORZENY going to England and that he would remain in the hands of the USEFT'.*

So in the end the US authorities did as they had been advised to do by that directive from the Joint Chiefs of Staff; they made an exception 'for intelligence and other military reasons'. In this way Eisenhower's reputation was protected. By 1948, however, when the Cold War was already looming large on the horizon, the chance offered itself in line with that 12 May 1945 directive to banish Skorzeny from the public gaze for good. It was that escape, supposedly engineered by former SS officers, and the mysterious Odessa organisation, which set up the 'ratlines' for Nazi escapers through Italy and thence to South America. But who had provided these SS officer, if they really were from the 'Black Guards', with the American licence plates, American uniforms and American ID? One can easily guess.

By the end of that year when he 'escaped' Skorzeny, under his new alias 'Rolf', was already working for the Gehlen Organization and indirectly for the new boys, the CIA. According to several published accounts, including one by former CIA agent Miles Copeland, Skorzeny helped to train the Egyptian Security Service for the Central Intelligence Agency. Later it was said that he worked for that same organisation when they were busily attempting to kill Fidel Castro in Cuba.

In 1951, while Skorzeny was still being sought by the German authorities for possible prosecution on war crimes charges, he was meeting an unnamed American Intelligence agent in Madrid. According to the US Air Force memo which records the encounter, the American

*US Forces, Europe Theater.

150

agent was on good terms with Skorzeny. 'Customary greeting is not unlike being welcomed by a huge bear or engulfed by a Saint Bernard dog,' reads the agent's report.

During the meeting Skorzeny complained that the US Treasury had frozen the profits from the American sales of his book of war memoirs, published about that time. This shocked his wife Countess Ilsa von Finkelstein. As the memo records: '[She exclaimed] Good God, do you realise that by our money going to the US Treasury, Rolf is actually paying for re-arming the French!'

In that same year, Eisenhower finally decided he would leave the command of NATO and run for the presidency. 'I LIKE IKE' was born. A year later the 'captive hero' was – unsurprisingly – President-elect. Ironically enough, the man who had once allegedly attempted to kill him was now the new President's employee.

Postscript:
And the Killing Went On?

On Monday 21 May 1945 men of the 51st Highland Division were busy screening Germans and foreign nationals, mainly 'displaced persons', attempting to go west over a small bridge near newly conquered Bremervoerde, Germany. They were on the look-out for war criminals and members of Himmler's SS who came under the 'automatic arrest' category. It was a boring job, but better than getting shot at, which had been their lot right up to two weeks before. So bored or not, they did their job conscientiously enough.

Some time that day the soldiers on the little bridge spotted three men in civilian clothes who seemed to be hesitant about crossing. They stood out immediately, not only because of their hesitancy but because some of them were obviously soldiers in civilian clothes. They could be SS. It was, however, the third man of the trio who caused the Jocks to stop them. He was small and skinny. It appeared there was nothing especially soldierly about him save for the black patch he wore over his right eye. It made him look like a performer from some third rate amateur drama group.

The trio's papers were examined. They seemed okay. But still the Jocks weren't happy with the man with the black piratical patch, named, he said, Hinziger. They asked more questions. It was then that the biggest of the trio made his mistake. He started to shout and threaten. That was enough for the men of the 'Black Watch' who had been fighting the 'squareheads' since the Battle of El Alamein back in 1942. They arrested the three of them.

They were sent to a British Army holding camp for suspects at Barnstedt ten miles from the British 2nd Army HQ at Luneburg. Here they were stripped and searched for anything incriminating plus what the guards there called 'SS cough-drops', i.e. suicide pills. Nothing was found. Thereafter they were questioned under the leadership of the camp commandant, a captain code-named 'Sylvester' of the Reconnaissance Corps. In the end Hinziger's nerve broke. Proudly he told a British sergeant, 'I am Reich Minister Heinrich Himmler, head of the SS and I want to talk to Eisenhower', adding he had a letter for Field Marshal Montgomery, head of the British Army in Germany. 'And I'm Winston

Churchill!' the British non-com quipped cynically and in disbelief. All the same, Sylvester took Hinziger's claim seriously. Then, apart from Martin Bormann, Hitler's secretary, all the top Nazis had been accounted for in the West. Only Himmler was still on the run. He called Colonel Murphy, 2nd Army's Chief Intelligence Officer, and was told to bring 'Hinziger' in.

The final day in the life of the man who had once terrorised Europe had commenced.

Himmler, for this really was the Reichsführer SS Heinrich Himmler, was taken to a suburban house in the small town of Luneburg whence the first of the current British royal family had come one thousand years before. Here he was stripped and given a blanket to wear because he wouldn't put on a British uniform before being medically examined by a British doctor. Once more the medic was looking for 'SS cough-drops'. Again the British doctor found no sign of the so-called 'lethal pill'. While Murphy listened, Himmler ranted how he was too important to deal with 'underlings'. He wanted to talk to Eisenhower. From that he went on to the need for the Western Allies and the defeated Germans to band together to fight their current ally Russia before it was too late.

Watching all this, the British doctor started to have second thoughts. Himmler was too confident, too smug. It was as if he still had some last ace up his sleeve. He stopped the interrogation and asked Himmler to come over to the window where there was more light. He wanted to look into the German's mouth. It was then that Himmler must have realised the game was up. As the MO put his finger into Himmler's mouth and spotted the cyanide capsule, Himmler bit down hard. The MO yelled and pulled out his bitten finger in the same instant that Himmler swallowed the contents of the hidden 'cough-drop'.

Immediately there was chaos. Some British officers grabbed Himmler, turned the naked Reichsführer upside down and immersed his head in cold water. Later it was reported that the doctor threaded a needle through Himmler's tongue to stretch it out so that he could reach down to his gullet and pull out what was left of the poison there. To no avail. Himmler died in agony. That was that. They threw a grey Army blanket over the corpse, posted guards outside, locked the door and went to report the sensational news to higher authorities.*

For twenty-four hours the British placed a security blanket over the whole affair. The body was photographed, examined in every way, there was even a death mask taken. Then the time came to get rid of the 'scourge of German-Occupied Europe'. There was not going to be any post-war

---

*One of the author's contacts, a British Army nurse, managed to cut a lock off the dead man's head which she sent together with photos of local horses she had ridden to her mother for safekeeping. Her mother thought the hair clip came from one of the horses and threw it away. A vital clue was lost.

'Himmler cult'. Under the command of a major, Sergeant-Major Austen and four men were picked to bury the body in the woods of the so-called 'Luneburg Heath' where three weeks before the German Army had surrendered to Montgomery. It was a well-wooded, swampy area, once the favourite spot of weekenders from the big north German cities. Now empty, there were places enough for the burial party to inter the body far from prying eyes. This they did. The man who had been responsible for the deaths of millions was buried in an unmarked spot as one might bury a stray dog killed running across the dead straight roads of the area. It seemed very fitting that the senior sergeant, Sgt Major Austen, had once worked for his local council as a dustman before the war.* He was an expert in removing trash!

This is the official account of how Himmler died. A suicide who had killed himself with poison. For nearly sixty years only historians of the Third Reich had concerned themselves (if at all) with the manner of Heinrich Himmler's death. All of them had been content to accept the British Army's account that he had died in captivity by his own hand. That was until May 2005 when a minor book by an obscure historian appeared in London. It was *Himmler's Secret War*, written by Martin Allen, an Englishman.

In the last few pages of his book, Mr Allen maintained that he had discovered documents in the British National Archives at Kew near London that indicated that Himmler had not committed suicide. Instead he had been murdered on Churchill's orders. The latter had discussed the assassination of captured enemy leaders (such as Mussolini) who 'knew too much' with the US President before FDR's death.

The book aroused little interest and no British national daily would touch the story, although it would have made excellent copy and raised the sales figures tremendously. That was until *The Daily Telegraph* broke the tale with a three-page coverage of its own investigation into it on 2 July this year.

The Telegraph, which had daily sales running into millions, investigated Allen's claims that he or his researcher had stumbled across documents, overlooked hitherto by other historians. And what sensational finds they were. In fact they purported that with Churchill's connivance and agreement, three key members of his entourage, including a minister in his cabinet and an Earl, had had Himmler murdered. Why? Because he knew about the peace negotiations being carried out during wartime with that master of terror and the scourge of European Jewry, Himmler.

But the newspaper had its doubts. They commissioned an expert in

---

*Two years later flowers were found near the spot where Himmler had been buried. A party was sent by the British Army to check on it. The body (if they did find the right spot in that great wood) had vanished!

forensic science, Mrs Audrey Giles. She testified that although the paper on which these top secret documents were typed was genuine 1945 material, as was the typewriter used, the letterheads of these same documents had been created by a high resolution laser printer developed only in the 1990s. Moreover, the old typewriter of 1945 vintage had been used on the documents typed in two separate government departments, separated physically by thousands of yards. Hardly likely, naturally. In addition, one of the key figures' signature had been traced in, first in pencil before the ink-version had been used over the pencilled tracer.

Mr Allen was called to account by the *Telegraph*. He said he was shocked, 'I think I've been set up', he told the reporter. 'But I do not even know by whom. I was devastated.'

Immediately the National Archives went on the alert. How had these documents, if they were forgeries, been planted in the archives? Anyone who has used the facility knows that security there is tight. Then again, who would be interested at this stage in time of attempting to blacken Churchill's character and indirectly that of Roosevelt by planting these very incriminating documents in the archive for the innocent historian to find them?

We may never know! Perhaps it is simply a continuation – for whatever reason – of that secret war that commenced so long ago. For then, so many famous and infamous international military and political figures were threatened and actually done to death.

So what does a death on paper, one that never took place, matter? One thing is for certain. It is that terrorism at the top, which started so long ago is now here to stay.

Index